EXCEL

PROGRAMMING

2 Books In 1:

The Ultimate Collection to Learn Excel VBA & Excel Macros Step by Step

DAVID A. WILLIAMS

TABLE OF CONTENTS

Excel VBA

The Ultimate Beginner's Guide to Learn VBA Programming Step by Step

Excel Macros

The Ultimate Beginner's Guide to Learn Excel Macros Step-by-Step

EXCEL VBA

The Ultimate Beginner's Guide to Learn VBA Programming Step by Step

David A. Williams

Introduction

Most people use Microsoft Excel at work, and they often perform repetitive tasks. Excel VBA is an extremely helpful tool since it will help you automate mundane tasks like copying data. For this, you will need to create a function that will reduce manual work thereby increasing productivity. When you learn how to use VBA, you can learn how to manipulate and customize the data in an Excel sheet. This book covers some basic information about VBA including the different data types and variables that you can use to automate processes and functions.

This book will take you through some basic concepts of VBA and will help you master programming in Excel VBA. You will also learn how to source data in Excel from one worksheet or workbook to another without having to open the files. You can use these statements to make it easier for you to perform iterative tasks. If you want to understand how you can use VBA to improve the processes that you work on, you have come to the right place. This book will also help you learn more about how you can manipulate strings and handle any errors.

Many examples have been given across the book that will help you learn the concepts better. You should practice these examples before you write any new code. You can also use the examples in the book as a base to write larger programs.

I hope you gathered all the information you were looking for.

CHAPTER 1

What Can You Do With VBA?

VBA or Visual Basic for Applications is a combination of Microsoft Office Applications and Visual Basic which is an event-driven programming language developed by Microsoft. VBA allows you to automate numerous activities in any Microsoft application using a Macro. This helps a user save the time he or she spends to perform repetitive activities.

People use Excel VBA for multiple reasons including the following:

- Creating lists
- Creating forms and invoices
- Analyzing data
- Developing diagrams and charts using data
- Forecasting and Budgeting

There are many other tasks one can perform using Excel, but I am sure you understand what I am saying. In simple words, one can use Excel to perform different tasks since you can automate any function in Excel using VBA. For example, you may want to develop or create a program that you can use to extract or import some numbers or data, and then format that data to help you print a report. When you develop the code, you can assign the code or macro to a button or a command. This will help you complete the task in a few minutes instead of an hour.

Common Uses of VBA

There are many reasons why most companies and organizations use VBA at work. It is important to remember that it will take you some time to write the code to automate any process. Therefore, you will need to take some time out of your busy schedule and see what you can do with VBA. This section covers some of the common processes that most people use VBA for.

Automating Documents

Most people hate having to prepare a document, and it is worse when the documents that are prepared have the same content or information that must be sent to many people. In such instances, one can use the Mail Merge add-in in Excel. This add-in is used to automate a document or letter. Remember that you cannot use this option if you need to write individual emails or documents. If you need to write individual documents, you can use VBA to help you create a form that will include the necessary information. You can also include some checkboxes that a user can choose from to create or write a document.

Word processing is only one of the many tasks that you can automate using VBA. You can also write different macros or programs to help you automate some functions in a spreadsheet. For instance, you can extract data or information from the Internet onto a spreadsheet just by clicking a button. This will help you reduce the time you spend on copying the information from the Internet and pasting it in the spreadsheet in the required format.

Customizing Application Interfaces

Some features in an application do not necessarily have to make your work easier for you, and these features can be turned off. You cannot turn these features off if you need to use them occasionally for work. Therefore, instead of disabling this feature, you can write a code in VBA that will allow you to access only those features that you use for your work. For instance, you can write a program in VBA if there are some additional functions, like conditional formatting, that you will need to include in your worksheet.

You can always change the interface of an application so that it can work better for you. You can customize menu systems and toolbars, and can also change how some elements function in the interface if you want to improve the look of the application. You can also use multiple interfaces if you want to switch between different interfaces.

One of the most common uses of VBA is to improve computation speed. You can perform numerous calculations in a few seconds. You can also create equations, graphs, and functions using the data in a worksheet or workbook. There will be a need to make changes or modifications to the data in the worksheet or workbook, and we will cover these concepts a little later in the book. If there are some complicated equations in your workbook or worksheet, you can use VBA to build a code that will simplify that process. There are some iterative functions that you can use to perform these calculations.

There are cases when the numbers that you obtain through some calculations will not make too much sense. You will only be able to use the number once someone has decided what to do with it. If these decisions are repetitive, you can use VBA to write a program that will decide what to do with the number while you play Hearts on your laptop.

Adding new Application Features

Many vendors and developers never use the applications that they build. Therefore, these applications are often not up to date. You can either tweak those applications or develop new applications using VBA. You can use these new applications to complete your work in a few minutes or less. This will certainly impress your boss, and could probably lead to a promotion.

CHAPTER 2

Parts of the Program

You must follow a specific structure and syntax when you write a program in VBA. This will help the debugger understand what your code is trying to achieve. This chapter will help you understand the structural elements in a program.

Defining the Parts of a Program

A program contains every element that is required to complete a specific task. Programs can cross modules, class modules, and also create boundaries. The idea of a program came into existence when computers were first used. Programs are containers that hold specific code that is used to implement some features or perform some tasks that the user or an operating system must perform. People often have a hard time understanding what a program is since most software packages define it incorrectly. When you build or create a new project, you are not developing a new program. It is important to remember that one VBA project can include multiple programs.

Programming Blocks

Every program, including a VBA program, consists of some building blocks. Since programming is an abstract concept, most people use physical examples to explain how things work. You will need to know what the abstract elements are in a VBA program since you cannot write a program otherwise. This section will list the different elements of a VBA program.

Project

A project is used to contain the different class modules, forms and modules for a specific workbook. When it comes to Excel, a user can only view the project for the workbook that is currently open.

Module, Class Module and Forms

These elements contain the main parts of the program including procedures and class descriptions. One project can have multiple forms, modules, and class modules in it, and each of them should have a different name.

Function and Sub

The function and sub elements in a VBA program will hold all the individual lines of code. Functions will always return the value that any user requires, but a sub does not perform that action. Therefore, it is important that you allow the VBA editor to access a specific program using a Sub.

Statement

Most developers and experts call one line of code a statement.

Using the Macro Recorder

A macro recorder will allow you to record all the keystrokes and actions that you will perform when you use VBA in Excel. Remember that this will also record any incorrect keystrokes as well. This tool is often used to record any task like highlighting text or using filters.

A macro recorder can be used to perform the following tasks:

- Discover how Word performs certain tasks.
- Create a macro based on your actions.
- Help you create the basis for a more complex program.
- Decide how to break your program into tasks.

A macro recorder does not write the code for you in VBA. For example, you cannot use a macro recorder to create a program without writing some additional code. This holds for programs that require user input or for programs that are dependent on the environment and the data you use. For these tasks, you will need to add more code, but it is a good way to start developing a program. You can always get the basics of the program set by using a macro recorder.

- Start the Macro Recorder.
- Perform all the steps that you normally perform to accomplish a task.
- Stop the Macro Recorder.
- Save the macro when the Office application prompts you.
- Optionally, open the resulting macro and make any required changes.

We will look at a macro recorder in more detail later in the book.

Using Subs

You can reduce the complexity or size of the code by using a sub. This is a packaging method that is present in a Macro dialog box. You will always need to use a sub to begin the program unless the program you are writing is for a different purpose. You can also use a sub when you are writing programs that will perform specific tasks and not return any value. Subs can also be used to display some information, and it can be used to perform different tasks. It is important to remember that a sub can never return any value. You can, however, use arguments as a way to modify the information in a function by using a Sub. Alternatively, you can use global variables. A sub can be used to break a complex or large code into smaller segments or sections, which will make it easy for you and any other user to understand the code better.

Using Functions

Once you have worked extensively with the Sub procedure, you may avoid using a Function. Remember that you cannot solve every problem or automate every process using a sub. You will need to use Function for different problems when compared to a Sub. For example, you will need to use a Function if you want to return some value to the user after performing some calculations. A sub, on the other hand, is used when you want to access any external code.

A Function always returns a value, which makes it different from a Sub. It is for this reason that most programmers write functions to avoid writing repetitive code. To process a list of names, you might create a Function to process each name individually and then call that Function once for each name. The Function can provide the processed information as a return value. We will look at how we can use loops to write repetitive code.

You can also use a Function for public code that you do not want to list in the Macro dialog box. You normally do not see a Function listed in the Macro dialog box — this dialog box usually lists only Subs.

Comments

It is always a good idea to include comments in your code to help any user, including yourself, to understand the purpose behind the code.

Writing Basic Comments

Comments can be written in different ways. Some programmers write pseudo-comments against blocks of code since this is one of the easiest ways to use a comment. Developers always add comments to any program that they are writing since it will provide a user with an understanding of why a specific line of code was written. These comments also provide some information on the updates made to the program. This is when a developer begins to write better programs.

The most important comment that you should include in your code is why you are writing the program. It is important to explain to other users why your program was written in a specific way. You should never leave vague comments since that will not help a user understand why you chose the method you did to write the code. These comments will also help you when you decide to update the code you have written. Using the comments, you can also understand why you must update the code.

A good programmer should always include the mistakes that they made while writing the code. This will help another programmer understand what they should avoid doing to improve their code. These comments will also help you when you choose to update the program that you have written.

Knowing when to use Comments

It is always a good idea to use comments wherever you think you should include them. It is a difficult task to include a comment and type it out in the code window, but it is always good to do so to explain what the purpose of the program is. It will take you some time to write a good comment, and it may also be difficult since you may wonder why you wrote the program in a specific way. If you do not have a good number of comments in your program, you may be unable to update it since you have no idea what the purpose of a function is. There will come a time when you will need to write the code from scratch because you have no idea what you were trying to do.

Writing Good Comments

A comment is said to be good if any user can understand what it means. You should always avoid using jargon, and explain the function of the statement in simple terms. If you want to explain every line of code, you can do this since it will help another user understand why you chose to act in a specific way.

CHAPTER 3

Fundamentals Of VBA

VBA is a visual programming environment. That is, you see how your program will look before you run it. Its editor is very visual, using various windows to make your programming experience easy and manageable. You will notice slight differences in the appearance of the editor when you use it with Vista as compared to older or newer versions of Windows. Regardless of which version of Windows you use or which Office Product you use, the Visual Basic Editor has the same appearance, same functionality, and same items.

The IDE is like a word processor, database form or a spreadsheet. The IDE, like every other application editor, has special features that make it easy to work with data. Apart from that, the IDE can also be used to write special instructions that help with data manipulation and analysis. VBA will follow the instructions in the program. The IDE in VBA consists of a toolbar, menu system, a Properties window, a Project Explorer window and a Code window. Below is a summary of what each Window contains.

Project Explorer

This window provides a list of the items or objects that are in your project. These items contain the document elements that are present in a single file. This application exists within a file, which you will see in the Project Explorer window.

Properties

When you select an object, the Properties window will give you all the information you need about that object. For instance, this window will tell you whether the object is empty or whether there are some words in it.

Code

Eventually, you will need to write some code, which will make the application work. This window will contain the special words that will tell the editor what it needs to do. This space is analogous to a to-do list or an algorithm.

Looking at the VBA Toolbox

You will not have to write a program for every task that you want Excel to perform. The IDE also allows you to use forms, which are similar to the forms that you use to perform different tasks. In the case of VBA, you will decide what should appear on the form and also decide how the form should act when a user enters some data into the form. VBA allows you to use the toolbox to create a form. This toolbox contains controls used to create forms.

Each Toolbox button performs a unique task. For example, when you click one button, a text box may appear on the screen. If you click another button, a mathematical operation may take place.

Starting the Visual Basic Editor

One can start the Visual Basic Editor in different ways depending on the application you are using. The newer versions of the Office Product use a different approach when compared to the older versions.

- Step 1: Go to Option “View” on the toolbar.
- Step 2: In the drop-down list, select “Record Macro.”
- Step 3: The interface will open, and you can begin typing the code for the worksheet you are in.

Using Project Explorer

The Project Explorer will appear in the Project Explorer Window, and you can use this to interact with different objects that make up the project. Every project is an individual file that you can use to hold your program or at least some pieces of it. This project will reside in the Office document, which you are using. Therefore, when you open the document, you also open the project. We will look at how programs and projects interact with each other in later chapters. The Project Explorer works like the left pane in Windows Explorer.

The Project Explorer lists the different objects you are using in the project. These objects depend on the type of application you are working with. For example, if you are working with Word, you see documents and document templates. Likewise, if you are working with Excel, you will come across different workbooks and worksheets. Regardless of the type of application you work with, the Project Explorer will be used in the same way.

A project can contain modules, class modules and forms. Let us look at the description of these objects:

- Forms These contain some user interface elements that allow you to interact with a user and collect the necessary information.
- Modules - These contain the nonvisual parts of your code or application. For instance, you can use a module to store some calculations.

- Class modules - These contain objects that you want to develop, and you can use a class module to create new data types.

Working with Special Entries

You can sometimes see some special entries in the Project Explorer. For instance, when you work on a Word document, you will see a References folder that will contain the references that the Word document makes. This contains a list of templates that the document uses to format the data in the document.

In many cases, you cannot modify or manipulate the objects in the folders. This is the case when Word document objects use a Reference folder. This folder is only available to provide information. If you want to modify or develop a referenced template, you should look for the object in the Project Explorer window. We will not discuss these concepts in the book since you do not work with these often.

Using the Properties Window

Most objects that you select in the IDE in VBA always have properties that describe the objects in a specific way. The "Property values are up" section talks about the properties that you have not worked with before. The following section will provide more information about the Properties Window.

Understanding Property Types

A property will always describe the object. When you look at an object, you will assume something about the product depending on whether the object is red, yellow, or green. In the same way, every VBA object has a specific type. One of the most common types is text. The property of every form is text, and this text appears at the top or bottom of the form when a user opens it. Another common property type is a Boolean value.

Getting Help with Properties

Do not expect to memorize every property for every object that VBA applications can create. Experts themselves cannot remember the properties for objects in different VBA applications. If you want to learn more about a specific object or property, select the property and press F1. VBA will display a Help window that will describe the functions or the properties of the object.

Using the Code Window

The Code Window is the space where you will write the code for your application. This window works like every other text editor that you have used, except that you type according to the syntax. When you open the Code window, you will not be able to view the Project Explorer and Property windows. You can display the Project Explorer window and Property by following the path: View -> Project Explorer and View ->Properties Window commands.

Opening an Existing Code Window

Sometimes you will not have the time to complete the code for an application and will need to work on it later. You must look for the module you want to use in the Project Explorer, and click on that. This will open an existing code window. Double-click the name of the module that you want to enter. You will see the code in the IDE window. This Code window will also appear when you want to perform a variety of tasks.

Creating a New Code Window

When you want to develop a new module in an existing document or template, you should open a new code window by using the following path: Insert -> Module or Insert -> Class Module command. Once you save this class module or module, it will always be in the Project Explorer with every other module that is in your project.

It is easier to execute one line of code at a time to understand where you may have made an error. You can do this by using the Immediate Window. You will always find this window at the bottom of the IDE, and it will not contain any information until you type something in it.

A developer spends a lot of time using the immediate window to check if there are any errors in the applications they are developing. You can use the immediate window to check with VBA if the function you have written produces the required value. To try this feature, type String1 = "Hello World" in the Immediate window and then press Enter. Now type '? String1' and then press Enter. Here, you have asked the editor to create a variable called String1 and assign it a value of Hello World. You can use the '?' operator to check the value assigned to the variable String1.

CHAPTER 4

VBA, A Primer

Microsoft Office products like PowerPoint, Word, Outlook, FrontPage, Visio, Access, Project, Excel and some other third-party programs support VBA. If you have Microsoft Office on your device, you have VBA. VBA works similarly on all Microsoft products except for Access. The differences only relate to the specific objects of every application. For example, if you are using a spreadsheet object, you can only use it in Excel. VBA is currently based on VB 6.0, but there is a possibility that the future releases will migrate towards .net.

The focus of this book is how you can use VBA in Excel. VBA enhances the use of Excel by providing valuable features that you will not find with Excel formulas.

Macro Recorder

You can write macros in VBA in the same way that you would write code in VB. The concepts of structures, variables, expressions, subprocedures, etc. are the same for both VB and VBA. The problem with VBA is that you will need to refer to every object you are writing code for. For example, if you were writing code for a specific cell in a worksheet, you will need to refer to that specific cell in your code. You are often unaware of what the names of these objects are and the attributes that you can control. The Macro Recorder solves this problem.

The macro recorder helps you develop a new macro in Excel quickly and easily. You must start the recorder and perform the necessary actions. The macro recorder will write the code for you. Alternatively, you can also run the VBA editor, which will allow you to insert a new module. This will give you a blank sheet on which you can write your macro. If you have already written the macro, you do not have to insert a new module. You will only need to add code to an existing module.

You will need to make some changes to the code written by the macro recorder. This is important to do when you need to change the cell references from absolute to relative or when you need the user form to interact with the user. If you have read the earlier version of the book, you will be familiar with VBA in Excel and some of the syntaxes and structures. Additionally, you must understand the differences between relative and absolute addressing.

VBA is different from VB in the sense that it is not a standalone language. VBA can only run through another product. For example, every VBA application you write in Excel can only run within Excel. This means that you will need to run Excel, then load the macro after which the compiler will execute the macro. The VBA applications are all stored in the spreadsheet that they were written in. You can also store VBA application in a way that will allow you to refer to them in other worksheets or workbooks.

When the application is loaded into Excel, you can invoke the application in many ways. Let us look at a few ways to run the macro:

1. You can assign a key to the macro when you record the macro. You can then invoke the macro by pressing Ctrl- "key." If the key is "a," your shortcut will be Ctrl+a. You must remember that the macro shortcut will override the default meaning of

the Ctrl+a shortcut. You should also note that Ctrl/a and Ctrl/A are different.

2. You can either include an object or a button on the spreadsheet to call the macro. Go to the Forms window using the path Menu->View->Toolbars->Forms and select the command button. Now, draw the button on the spreadsheet. Choose the macro that you want to link to the button when the dialog box or prompt opens. You can also include pictures and other objects and assign macros to them.

3. Select the macro from the menu and run it. Go to the Macros section using the following path Menu->Tools->Macro->Macros and choose the macro you want to run.

4. You can also use the VBA editor to run the macro. You can either click on the run button to run the macro or go through each line of the code while giving yourself time to debug the code. When you are debugging the code, you should move the VBA editor into a pane adjacent to the spreadsheet and execute the code to see what is happening.

If you choose to name a macro "Sub Auto_Open()," this macro will run when you load or open the spreadsheet. This will only happen if you have enabled macros.

As mentioned in the previous chapter, the macro recorder is an important and useful tool in Excel. This tool will record every action that you perform in Excel. You only need to record a task once using the macro recorder, and you can execute that same task a million times by clicking a button. If you do not know how to program a specific task in Excel, you can use the Macro Recorder to help you understand what you need to do. You can then open the Visual Basic Editor once you have recorded the task to see how you can program it.

You cannot perform many tasks when you use the Macro Recorder. For instance, you cannot use the macro recorder to loop through data. The macro recorder also uses more code than you need, which will slow the process down.

Record A Macro

- Go to the Menu Bar and move the Developer Tab, and click the button to Record the Macro.
- Enter the name of the macro.
- Choose the workbook where you want to use the macro. This means that the macro can only be used in the current workbook.
- If you store the macro in a personal macro workbook, you can access the macro in all your workbooks. This is only because Excel stores the macro in a hidden workbook, which will open automatically when it starts. If you store the macro in a new workbook, you can use the macro only in the opened workbook.
- Click OK.
- Now, right click on the active cell in the worksheet. Ensure that you do not select any other cell. Click format cells.
- Select the percentage.
- Click OK.
- Now, select the stop recording.

You have successfully recorded your macro using the macro recorder.

Run The Recorded Macro

You will now need to test the macro and see if you can change the format of the numbers to percentage.

- Enter any numbers between 0 and 1 in the spreadsheet.
- Select the numbers.
- Move to the Developer tab, and click Macros.
- Now click run.

See The Macro

If you want to look at the macro, you should open the Visual Basic Editor.

The macro, called Module 1, is placed in a module. The code that is placed in the module is always available to the full workbook. This means you can change the format for the numbers in all the sheets in the workbook. If you assign a macro to the command button, you should remember that the macro would only be available for that specific sheet.

Security and Macro Storage

For every Microsoft Office application, there are three security levels for macros. The macro security level is always set to high by default. To change the security of your macro, go to the security tab and make your selection. Go to Menu->Tools->Security Tab->Macro Security.

The three security levels for macros are:

1. High: The macros that are signed by a trusted source will run in Excel. If there is any unsigned macro, it will automatically be disabled.

2. Medium: This is the recommended setting since you can choose to enable or disable a macro.

3. Low: This is not recommended since the macros are loaded into the workbook without notifying the user.

If you know you will be using macros, you should set the security of the macros to medium. When you load the spreadsheet, Excel will ask you if you want to enable or disable a macro. If you know that a specific sheet contains a macro and you know who wrote it, you can enable it.

Since some macros are set to run when you open a spreadsheet, it is not possible for you to always have the chance to examine the macro before you enable it. It is important to remember that an Excel Macro virus is very rare. This is because a macro is only available on the spreadsheet where it was written. Macros are always stored in the workbook by default and every time you load the workbook, and the macros are loaded.

When you create a macro for the first time, you can decide where to store the macro. The best choices are:

1. This Workbook: The macro is stored in the worksheet where it is written. Anybody who has access to the worksheet can access the macro.

2. Personal Macro Workbook: All the macros on your PC are stored in this workbook. Only when you copy the macro and save it with the spreadsheet will others be able to view the macro.

You can use the VBA editor to see where the macros are stored. The Project Explorer Window, on the upper left of the screen, shows you where the files are placed and their hierarchy. You can use the Explorer to view, move, copy or delete a macro.

How To Add A Trusted Location

As mentioned earlier, you can save the workbooks with macros in a folder that you mark as a trusted location. If you save a workbook in that folder, the macros will always be enabled. The developers suggest that you should always have a trusted location in your hard drive. Remember that you can never trust the location on a network drive.

If you want to specify a trusted location, you should follow the steps given below:

1. Go to the Developer Tab and click on Macro Security.
2. Move to the left navigation pane in the Trust Center and choose the Trusted Location.
3. If you want to save the file on a network drive, you should add that location into the trusted locations.
4. Go to 'My Networks' in the Trusted Location dialog box and click the 'Add New Location' button.
5. You will see the list of Trusted Locations in a dialog box.
6. Now click the Browse button and go to the parent folder of the folder that you want to make a trusted location. Now click on the Trusted Folder. You will not find the name of the Folder in the text box, but click OK. The correct name will come in the Browse dialog box.
7. If you want to include the subfolders in the selected folder, you should select the radio button against the 'Subfolders of this location are also trusted' option.
8. Now, click OK to add the folder to the list.

How To Enable Macros Outside A Trusted Location

When you do not save an Excel workbook in a trusted location, excel will always rely on the macro settings. In Excel 2003, a macro could have a low, medium, high or very high security. These settings were later renamed by the developers in Microsoft. If you want to access the macro settings, you should go to the Developers Tab and choose Macro Security. Excel will then display the Macro Settings dialog box. You should select the 'Disable All Macros with Notification' option. Let us look at the description of the options in the dialog box.

Disable All Macros Without Notification

This setting will not allow any macro to run. If you do not always want to run the macro when you open the workbook, you should choose this setting. However, since you are still learning how to use macros and work with them, you should not use this setting. This setting is equivalent to the Very High Security that is found in Excel 2003. If you choose this setting, you can only run macros if they are saved in a Trusted Location.

Disable All Macros With Notification

This setting is like the Medium security setting in Excel 2003. This is the recommended setting that you should use. If you use this setting, Excel will ask you if you want to enable to disable a macro when you open a workbook. You may often choose this option if you are a beginner. In Excel 2010, you will see a message in the message area, which states that the macros have been disabled. You can either choose to enable or disable the content in the workbook by choosing that option.

Disable All Macros Except Digitally Signed Macros

If you wish to use this setting, you should always use a digital signing tool like VeriSign or any other provider to sign your macro. If you are going to sell your macros to other parties, you should use this security option. This is a hassle if you want to write macros only for your use.

Enable All Macros

Experts suggest that you do not use this option since dangerous codes can also run on your system. This setting is equivalent to the Low-security option in Excel 2003 and is the easiest option to use. This option will open your system up to attacks from malicious viruses.

Disabling All Macros With Notification

Experts suggest that you set your macro to disable all content after it gives you a notification. If you save a workbook with a macro using this setting, you will see a security warning right above the formula bar when you open the workbook. If you know that there are macros in the workbook, all you need to do is click 'Enable Content.' You can click on the X on the far right of the bar if you do not want to enable any of the macros in the workbook.

If you do forget to enable the macro and then attempt to run that macro, Excel will indicate that the macro will not run since you have disabled all macros in the workbook. If this happens, you should reopen the workbook to enable the macros again.

CHAPTER 5

Working With Loops

One of the most powerful and basic programming tools available in VBA is a loop. This tool is used across many programming languages where the programmer wants to repeat a block of code until a condition holds true or until a specific point. If the condition is false, the loop will break and the section of code after the loop is executed. By using loops, you can write a few lines of code and achieve significant output.

The For Loop

For Loop

Most people use the For Loop in VBA. There are two forms of the For Loop – For Next and For Each In Next. The For Loop will move through a series of data in a sequence. You can use the Exit statement to end the For Loop at any point. The loop will continue to run until the condition is met. When the final condition is met, the editor will move to the next statement in the program, which is the natural direction.

Let us look at the syntax of the loop:

The For … Next loop has the following syntax:

```
For counter = start_counter To end_counter

'Do something here (your code)

Next counter
```

In the syntax above, we are initializing the counter variable, which will maintain the loop. This counter variable will be set to a value that is equal to the start_counter that will be the beginning of the loop. This variable will increase in number until it meets the end condition which is the end_counter variable. The loop will continue to run until the value of the counter is equal to the value of the end_counter variable. This loop will execute once until the values match, after which the loop will stop.

The explanation above can be slightly confusing, therefore let us look at a few examples that you can use to understand the For Loop better. Before we look at the examples, follow the steps given below:

Open a new workbook and save it using the .xlsm extension.

Now, press Alt+F11 to launch the Visual Basic Editor screen.

Now, insert a new module.

Example 1

[1]In this example, we will display a number using a message box.

```
Sub Loop1()

Dim StartNumber As Integer
```

---

[1] 7 Examples of For Loops in Microsoft Excel VBA | VBA. (2019). Retrieved from https://www.exceltip.com/vba/for-loops-with-7-examples.html

```
Dim EndNumber As Integer

EndNumber = 5

        For StartNumber = 1 To EndNumber

        MsgBox StartNumber & " is " & "Your StartNumber"

        Next StartNumber

End Sub
```

In the above code, the StartNumber and EndNumber variables are declared as integers, and the StartNumber is the start of your loop. The values that you enter in the loop can be anywhere in between the StartNumber and EndNumber. The code will start from StartNumber, which is 1, and end at EndNumber which is 5. Once the code runs, the following message will be displayed on the screen.

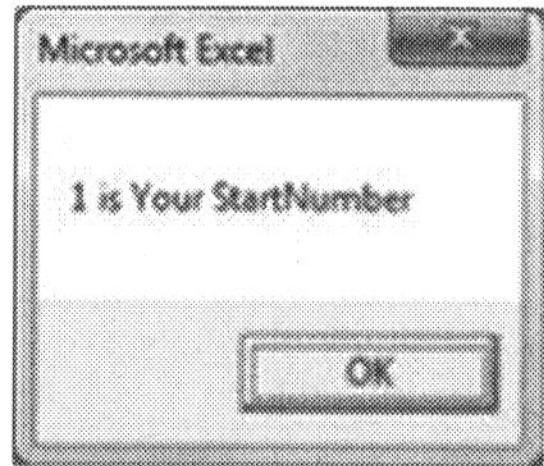

Example 2

[2]In this example, we will fill values in the Active worksheet.

```
Sub Loop2()

'Fills cells A1:A56 with values of X by looping' --- Comment
```

---

[2] 7 Examples of For Loops in Microsoft Excel VBA | VBA. (2019). Retrieved from https://www.exceltip.com/vba/for-loops-with-7-examples.html

```
'Increase the value of X by 1 in each loop' --- Comment

Dim X As Integer

   For X = 1 To 56

         Range("A" & X).Value = X

         Next X

End Sub
```

You will see the following output.

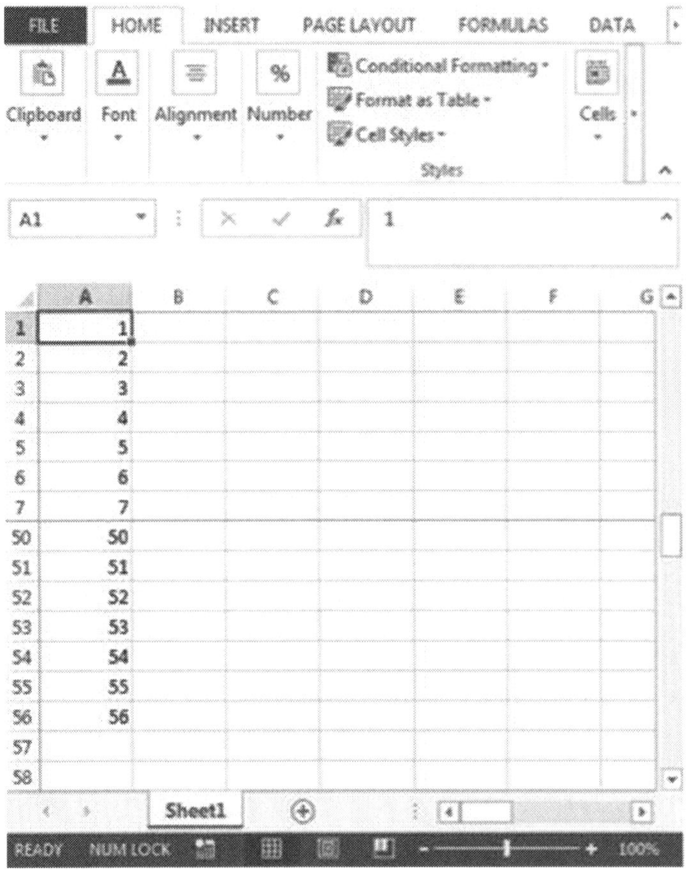

For…Next Statement

The For…Next Loop[3] will repeat a statement or a block of code for a specific number of iterations. The syntax for the loop is as follows:

```
For counter_variable = start_value To end_value

[block of code]

Next counter_variable
```

Let us look at a simple example of how to use this loop.

```
Sub forNext1()

Dim i As Integer

Dim iTotal As Integer

iTotal = 0

For i = 1 To 5

iTotal = i + iTotal

Next i

MsgBox iTotal

End Sub
```

The For Each … Next Statement

If you want to repeat a block of code for every object or variable in a group, you should use the For Each…Next Loop. This statement will

---

[3] 7 Examples of For Loops in Microsoft Excel VBA | VBA. (2019). Retrieved from https://www.exceltip.com/vba/for-loops-with-7-examples.html

repeat the execution of a block of code or statements for every element in the collection. The loop will stop when every element in the collection is covered. The execution will immediately move to that section of code that is immediately after the Next statement. The syntax of the loop is as follows:

```
For Each object_variable In group_object_variable

[block of code]

Next object_variable
```

Example 1

[4]In the example below, the loop will go through every worksheet in the workbook. VBA will execute the code which will protect the worksheets with a password. In this example, the variable ws is the Worksheet Object variable. The group or collection of worksheets is present in this workbook.

```
Sub forEach1()

Dim ws As Worksheet

For Each ws In ThisWorkbook.Worksheets

ws.Protect Password:="123"

Next ws

End Sub
```

---

[4] 7 Examples of For Loops in Microsoft Excel VBA | VBA. (2019). Retrieved from https://www.exceltip.com/vba/for-loops-with-7-examples.html

Example 2

[5]In the example below, the VBA will iterate through every cell in the range A1:A10. The code will set the background color of every cell to yellow. In this example, rCell is the Range Object variable, and the collection or group of cells is present in Range(“A1:A10”).

```
Sub forEach2()

Dim rCell As Range

For Each rCell In ActiveSheet.Range("A1:A10")

rCell.Interior.Color = RGB(255, 255, 0)

Next rCell

End Sub
```

Nesting Loops

If you want to include more than one condition in a loop, you can use nesting. You can create a nested loop by adding one loop to another. You can add an infinite number of loops if you are creating a nested loop. You can also nest one type of a loop inside another type of loop.

If you are using a For Loop, it is important that the inner loop is completed first. It is only after the inner loop is fully complete that the statements below the Next statement of the inner loop are executed. Alternatively, you can nest one type of control structure in another.

---

[5] 7 Examples of For Loops in Microsoft Excel VBA | VBA. (2019). Retrieved from https://www.exceltip.com/vba/for-loops-with-7-examples.html

In the example below, we will use an IF statement in a WITH statement that is within a For...Each Loop. VBA will go through every cell in the range A1:A10. If the value of the cell exceeds 5, VBA will color the cell as Yellow. Otherwise, it will color the cells red.

```
Sub nestingLoops()

Dim rCell As Range

For Each rCell In ActiveSheet.Range("A1:A10")

With rCell

If rCell > 5 Then

.Interior.Color = RGB(255, 255, 0)

Else

.Interior.Color = RGB(255, 0, 0)

End If

End With

Next rCell

End Sub
```

The Exit For Statement

The Exit For statement can be used to exit the For Loop without completing the full cycle. This means that you will be exiting the For Loop early. This statement will instruct VBA to stop the execution of the loop and move to the section or block of code at the end of the loop, or the code that follows the Next statement. In the case that you are using a Nested Loop, the VBA compiler will stop executing the code in the inner loop, and begin to execute the statements in the outer loop. You should use this statement when you want to terminate the loop once it has satisfied a condition or reached a specific value. This statement can also be used to break an endless loop after a certain point.

Let us look at the following example:

In the example below, if the value of Range("A1") is blank, the value of the variable iTotal will be 55. If Range("A1") has the value 5, VBA will terminate the loop when the counter reaches the value 5. At this point, the value of iTotal will be 15. You should note that the loop will run until the counter value reaches 5, after which it will exit the loop.

```
Sub exitFor1()

Dim i As Integer

Dim iTotal As Integer

iTotal = 0

For i = 1 To 10

iTotal = i + iTotal

If i = ActiveSheet.Range("A1") Then

Exit For

End If

Next i

MsgBox iTotal

End Sub
```

Do...Loop Statement

We have at what the Do…Loop statement is and how you can use it in Excel VBA. We will now look at the syntax and understand every part of the syntax. There are some examples and exercises in this section that will help you master the Do…Loop statement.

Syntax

Type 1

```
Do { While | Until } condition
        [ statements ]
        [ Continue Do ]
        [ statements ]
        [ Exit Do ]
        [ statements ]
Loop
```

Type 2

```
Do
        [ statements ]
        [ Continue Do ]
        [ statements ]
        [ Exit Do ]
        [ statements ]
Loop { While | Until } condition
```

Understanding The Parts

Term	Definition
Do	This term is necessary to include since this starts the Do Loop.
While	This is required unless you use UNTIL in the loop. This keyword will ensure that the editor runs the loop until the condition is false.
Until	This keyword is necessary unless you are using the WHILE keyword. This will ensure that the editor will run the loop until the condition holds true.
Condition	This is optional, but it should always be a Boolean expression. If the condition is nothing, the editor will treat it as false.
Statements	These are optional. You can add one or more statements that you want the editor to repeat until the condition holds true.
Continue Do	This is also an optional statement. If you use this statement in the loop, the editor will move to the next iteration of the loop.
Exit Do	This is optional, and if you use it, the editor will move out of the Do Loop.
Loop	This keyword is necessary since it terminates the loop.

You should use the Do...Loop structure if you want to repeat a set of statements infinitely until the condition holds true. If you want to repeat the statements in the loop for a specific number of times, you should use the For...Next statements. You can either use the Until or While keywords when you specify a condition, but you should never use both.

You can place the condition either at the start or at the end of the loop. The first book mentions which structure you should use depending on when you want to test the condition. If you want to test the condition at the beginning, the loop does not have to run even once. If you test the condition at the end of the loop, the statements in the body of the loop will run at least once. This condition is a Boolean value and is often a comparison of two values. These values can be of any data type that the editor can convert to Boolean.

You can nest a Do loop by adding another loop in it. You can also nest different control structures within the Do Loop. These concepts have been covered in the first book of the series.

You should remember that the Do...Loop structure is more flexible than the While...End While statement. This is because the former allows you to decide if you want to end the loop when the condition first becomes true or when it stops being true. You also can test the condition either at the start or the end of the loop.

Exit Do

You can use the Exit Do statement as an alternative way to exit the Do...Loop. The VBA Compiler will now execute the statements that are written immediately after the loop. The Exit Do is used if you nest conditional statements within the loop. If you know that there is some condition that is unnecessary or makes it impossible for the editor to evaluate the statements within the loop. You can use this statement if you want to check for a condition that can lead to an endless loop.

This statement will help you exit the loop immediately. You can use any number of Exit Do statements in the Do…Loop structure.

When you use the Exit Do statement in a nest Do loop, the editor will move from the statements within the innermost loop to the next level of nesting statements.

Example 1

[6]In the example below, the editor will run the statements in the loop only when the index variable is greater than 10. The Until keyword will end the loop.

```
Dim index As Integer = 0

Do

        Debug.Write(index.ToString & " ")

        index += 1

Loop Until index > 10

Debug.WriteLine("")
```

The output will be,

0 1 2 3 4 5 6 7 8 9 10

Example 2

---

[6] Do...Loop Statement (Visual Basic). (2019). Retrieved from https://docs.microsoft.com/en-us/dotnet/visual-basic/language-reference/statements/do-loop-statement

[7]In the example below, we will use a While clause instead of the Until clause. The editor will test the condition at the start of the loop.

```
Dim index As Integer = 0

Do While index <= 10

        Debug.Write(index.ToString & " ")

        index += 1

Loop

Debug.WriteLine("")
```

The output will be,

0 1 2 3 4 5 6 7 8 9 10

The Do While Loop

You can use the Do While Loop to repeat a block of code or statements indefinitely as long as the value of the condition holds true. VBA will stop executing the block of code when the condition returns the value False. The condition can either be tested at the start or at the end of the loop. The Do While...Loop statement is where the condition is tested at the start while the Do...Loop While the statement is the condition that is tested at the end of the loop. When the condition at the start of the loop is not met, the former loop will not execute the block of code in the loop. The latter statement will function at least once since the condition is at the end of the loop.

---

[7] Do...Loop Statement (Visual Basic). (2019). Retrieved from https://docs.microsoft.com/en-us/dotnet/visual-basic/language-reference/statements/do-loop-statement

Do While…Loop Statement

The syntax for the loop is:

Do While [Condition]

[block of code]

Loop

Do…Loop While Statement

The syntax for the loop is:

Do

[block of code]

Loop While [Condition]

The loops are explained below with the help of examples.

Example 1

[8]In the example below, the condition is tested at the beginning of the loop. Since the condition is not met, the loop will not execute, and the value of iTotal will be zero.

Sub doWhile1()

Dim i As Integer

Dim iTotal As Integer

---

[8] Do...Loop Statement (Visual Basic). (2019). Retrieved from https://docs.microsoft.com/en-us/dotnet/visual-basic/language-reference/statements/do-loop-statement

```
i = 5

iTotal = 0

Do While i > 5

iTotal = i + iTotal

i = i - 1

Loop

MsgBox iTotal

End Sub
```

Example 2

[9]In the example below, the condition is only tested at the end of the function. Since the condition is true, the loop will execute once. It will terminate after that since the value of I will reduce to 4, and the variable iTotal will return the value 5.

```
Sub doWhile2()

Dim i As Integer

Dim iTotal As Integer

i = 5

iTotal = 0

Do
```

---

[9] Do...Loop Statement (Visual Basic). (2019). Retrieved from https://docs.microsoft.com/en-us/dotnet/visual-basic/language-reference/statements/do-loop-statement

```
iTotal = i + iTotal

i = i - 1

Loop While i > 5

MsgBox iTotal

End Sub
```

Example 3

[10]In this example, we will replace the blanks in a range of cells with underscores.

```
Sub doWhile3()

Dim rCell As Range

Dim strText As String

Dim n As Integer

'rCell is a Cell in the specified Range which contains the strText

'strText is the text in a Cell in which blank spaces are to be replaced with underscores

'n is the position of blank space(s) occurring in a strText

For Each rCell In ActiveSheet.Range("A1:A5")

strText = rCell
```

---

[10] Do...Loop Statement (Visual Basic). (2019). Retrieved from https://docs.microsoft.com/en-us/dotnet/visual-basic/language-reference/statements/do-loop-statement

'the VBA InStr function returns the position of the first occurrence of a string within another string. Using this to determine the position of the first blank space in the strText.

n = InStr(strText, " ")

Do While n > 0

'blank space is replaced with the underscore character in the strText

strText = Left(strText, n - 1) & "_" & Right(strText, Len(strText) - n)

'Use this line of code instead of the preceding line, to remove all blank spaces in the strText

'strText= Left(strText, n - 1) & Right(strText, Len(strText) - n)

n = InStr(strText, " ")

Loop

rCell = strText

Next

End Sub

The Exit Do Statement

The Exit Do Statement can be used to exit the Do While Loop before you complete the cycle. The Exit Do statement will instruct VBA to stop executing the lines of code in the loop and move to the block of code that is immediately after the loop. If it is a nested loop, the statement will instruct VBA to execute the lines of code in the outer loop. You can use an infinite number of Exit Do statements in a loop, and this statement is useful when you want to terminate the loop once you obtain the desired value. This is similar to the Exit For statement.

Let us look at the following example[11]. In this example, the block of code will not be executed if the cell A1 contains a number between 0 and 11 since the condition states that the loop should be terminated if the value of 'i' is equal to the value in Cell A1.

```
Sub exitDo1()

Dim i As Integer

Dim iTotal As Integer

iTotal = 0

Do While i < 11

iTotal = i + iTotal

i = i + 1

If i = ActiveSheet.Range("A1") Then

Exit Do

End If

Loop

MsgBox iTotal

End Sub
```

The Do Until Loop

---

[11] Do...Loop Statement (Visual Basic). (2019). Retrieved from https://docs.microsoft.com/en-us/dotnet/visual-basic/language-reference/statements/do-loop-statement

The block of code in the Do Until loop is executed repeatedly until a specific condition is true. You can test the condition in the system either at the start or at the end of the loop. The Do Until Loop statement will test the condition at the start of the loop while the Do Loop Until Statement will test the condition at the end of the loop. In the former statement, the block of code within the loop is not executed even once if the condition is false. This means that the condition must hold true from the start. In the latter statement, the block of code within the loop will execute at least once even if the condition is false since the condition is at the end of the loop.

Do Until…Loop Statement

The syntax for the statement is below:

Do Until [Condition]

[block of code]

Loop

Do…Loop Until Statement

The syntax for the statement is below:

Do

[block of code]

Loop Until [Condition]

Let us understand these statements better using the following examples:

Example 1

[12]In this example, we are instructing VBA to color a blank cell until the compiler reaches a non-empty cell. If the first cell is a non-empty cell, the code in the body of the loop will not be executed since the condition is mentioned at the start of the loop.

```
Sub doUntil1()

Dim rowNo As Integer

rowNo = 1

Do Until Not IsEmpty(Cells(rowNo, 1))

Cells(rowNo, 1).Interior.Color = RGB(255, 255, 0)

rowNo = rowNo + 1

Loop

End Sub
```

Example 2

[13]In this example, we are instructing VBA to color a blank cell until the compiler reaches a non-empty cell. If the first cell is a non-empty cell, the code in the body of the loop will only be executed once because the condition is only mentioned at the end of the loop.

---

12 Do...Loop Statement (Visual Basic). (2019). Retrieved from https://docs.microsoft.com/en-us/dotnet/visual-basic/language-reference/statements/do-loop-statement

13 Do...Loop Statement (Visual Basic). (2019). Retrieved from https://docs.microsoft.com/en-us/dotnet/visual-basic/language-reference/statements/do-loop-statement

```
Sub doUntil2()

Dim rowNo As Integer

rowNo = 1

Do

Cells(rowNo, 1).Interior.Color = RGB(255, 255, 0)

rowNo = rowNo + 1

Loop Until Not IsEmpty(Cells(rowNo, 1))

End Sub
```

The Exit Do Statement

You can exit the Do Until loop without executing all the commands in the body of the loop using the Exit Do statement. This function is similar to what was done in the Do While Loop.

CHAPTER 6

Working With Conditional Statements

There are two conditional statements that you can use in VBA:

1. If…Then…Else
2. Select…Case

In both these conditional statements, VBA will need to evaluate one or more conditions after which the block of code between the parentheses is executed. These statements are executed depending on what the result of the evaluation is.

If…Then…Else Statements

This conditional statement will execute a block of statements or code when the condition is met.

Multiple-line Statements

If condition Then

statements

ElseIf elseif_condition_1 Then

elseif_statements_1

ElseIf elseif_condition_n Then

elseif_statements_n

Else

else_statements

End If

Let us break the statements down to understand what each part of the block of code written above means.

If Statement

If you want to write a multiple-line syntax, like the example above, the first line of the code should only contain the 'If' statement. We will cover the single-line syntax in the following section.

Condition

This is an expression that could either be a string or numeric. The compiler will evaluate this condition and return either true or false. It is necessary to define a condition.

Statements

These statements make up the block of code that the compiler will execute if the condition is true. If you do not specify a statement, then the compiler will not execute any code even if the condition is true.

ElseIf

This is a clause that can be used if you want to include multiple conditions. If you have an ElseIf in the code, you need to specify the elseif_condition. You can include an infinite number of ElseIf and elseif_conditions in your code.

elseif_condition

This is an expression that the compiler will need to evaluate. The result of the expression should either be true or false.

Elseif_statements

These statements or blocks of code are evaluated if the compiler returns the result true for the elseif_condition. If you do not specify a statement, then the compiler will not execute any code even if the condition is true.

The Else -> condition and elseif_conditions are always tested in the order they are written in. The code that is written immediately after a condition is executed if the condition holds true. If no conditions in the elseif_conditions returns the value the true, the block of code after the **Else** clause will be executed. You can choose to include the Else in the If…Then…Else statement.

else_statements

These statements are the blocks of code written immediately after the Else statement.

End If

This statement terminates the execution of the statements in the If…Then…Else block of code. It is essential that you use these keywords only at the end of the block of code.

Nesting

You can nest the If…Then…Else statements in a loop using the Select…Case or VBA Loops (covered in the previous chapter), without a limit. If you are using Excel 2003, you can only nest loops seven times, but if you use Excel 2007, you can use 64. The latest versions of Excel allow a larger level of nesting.

Let us look at the following example:

Example 1

[14]

```
Sub ElseIfStructure()

'Returns Good if the marks are equal to 60.

Dim sngMarks As Single

sngMarks = 60

If sngMarks >= 80 Then

MsgBox "Excellent"

ElseIf sngMarks >= 60 And sngMarks < 80 Then

MsgBox "Good"

ElseIf sngMarks >= 40 And sngMarks < 60 Then

MsgBox "Average"

Else

MsgBox "Poor"

End If

End Sub
```

---

[14] Conditional Statements in Excel VBA - If, Case, For, Do Loops. (2019). Retrieved from https://analysistabs.com/excel-vba/conditional-statements/

Example 2

In this example, we will use Multiple If…Then Statements. This is an alternative to the ElseIf structure, but is not as efficient as the ElseIf Structure. In the Multiple If…Then Statements, the compiler will need to run through every If…Then block of code even after it returns the result true for one of the conditions. If you use the ElseIf structure, the subsequent conditions are not checked if one condition is true. This makes the ElseIf structure faster. If you can perform the function using the ElseIf structure, you should avoid using the Multiple If…Then Structure.

```
Sub multipleIfThenStmnts()

''Returns Good if the marks are equal to 60.

Dim sngMarks As Single

sngMarks = 60

If sngMarks >= 80 Then

MsgBox "Excellent"

End If

If sngMarks >= 60 And sngMarks < 80 Then

MsgBox "Good"

End If

If sngMarks >= 40 And sngMarks < 60 Then

MsgBox "Average"

End If

If sngMarks < 40 Then
```

MsgBox "Poor"

End If

End Sub

Example 3

In this example, we will nest the If…Then…Else statements within a For…Next Loop.

Sub IfThenNesting()

'The user will need to enter 5 numbers. The compiler will add the even numbers and subtract the odd numbers.

Dim i As Integer, n As Integer, iEvenSum As Integer, iOddSum As Integer

For n = 1 To 5

i = InputBox("enter number")

If i Mod 2 = 0 Then

iEvenSum = iEvenSum + i

Else

iOddSum = iOddSum + i

End If

Next n

MsgBox "sum of even numbers is " & iEvenSum

MsgBox "sum of odd numbers is " & iOddSum

End Sub

Example 4

You can use the following options to test multiple variables using the If…Then statements.

Option 1: ElseIf Structure

```
Sub IfThen1()

'this procedure returns the message "Pass in maths and Fail in science"

Dim sngMaths As Single, sngScience As Single

sngMaths = 50

sngScience = 30

If sngMaths >= 40 And sngScience >= 40 Then

MsgBox "Pass in both maths and science"

ElseIf sngMaths >= 40 And sngScience < 40 Then

MsgBox "Pass in maths and Fail in science"

ElseIf sngMaths < 40 And sngScience >= 40 Then

MsgBox "Fail in maths and Pass in science"

Else

MsgBox "Fail in both maths and science"

End If

End Sub
```

Option 2: If…Then…Else Nesting

```
Sub IfThen2()

'this procedure returns the message "Pass in maths and Fail in science"

Dim sngMaths As Single, sngScience As Single

sngMaths = 50

sngScience = 30

If sngMaths >= 40 Then

If sngScience >= 40 Then

MsgBox "Pass in both maths and science"

Else

MsgBox "Pass in maths and Fail in science"

End If

Else

If sngScience >= 40 Then

MsgBox "Fail in maths and Pass in science"

Else

MsgBox "Fail in both maths and science"

End If

End If

End Sub
```

Option 3: Multiple If…Then Statements

As mentioned earlier, this may not be the best way to perform the operation.

```
Sub IfThen3()

'this procedure returns the message "Pass in maths and Fail in science"

Dim sngMaths As Single, sngScience As Single

sngMaths = 50

sngScience = 30

If sngMaths >= 40 And sngScience >= 40 Then

MsgBox "Pass in both maths and science"

End If

If sngMaths >= 40 And sngScience < 40 Then

MsgBox "Pass in maths and Fail in science"

End If

If sngMaths < 40 And sngScience >= 40 Then

MsgBox "Fail in maths and Pass in science"

End If

If sngMaths < 40 And sngScience < 40 Then

MsgBox "Fail in both maths and science"

End If

End Sub
```

Example 5

In this example, we will use the If Not, If IsNumeric and IsEmpty functions in the Worksheet_Change event.

Private Sub Worksheet_Change(ByVal Target As Range)

'Using If IsEmpty, If Not and If IsNumeric (in If…Then statements) in the Worksheet_Change event.

'auto run a VBA code, when content of a worksheet cell changes, with the Worksheet_Change event.

On Error GoTo ErrHandler

Application.EnableEvents = False

'if target cell is empty post change, nothing will happen

If IsEmpty(Target) Then

Application.EnableEvents = True

Exit Sub

End If

'using If Not statement with the Intersect Method to determine if Target cell(s) is within specified range of "B1:B20"

If Not Intersect(Target, Range("B1:B20")) Is Nothing Then

'if target cell is changed to a numeric value

If IsNumeric(Target) Then

'changes the target cell color to yellow

Target.Interior.Color = RGB(255, 255, 0)

```
End If

End If

Application.EnableEvents = True

ErrHandler:

        Application.EnableEvents = True

        Exit Sub

End Sub
```

Using the Not Operator

When you use the Not operator on any Boolean expression, the compiler will reverse the true value with the false value and vice versa. The Not operator will always reverse the logic in any conditional statement. In the example above, If Not Intersect(Target, Range("B1:B20")) Is Nothing Then means If Intersect(Target, Range("B1:B20")) Is Not Nothing Then or If Intersect(Target, Range("B1:B20")) Is Something Then. In simple words, this means that the condition should not be true if the range falls or intersects between the range ("B1:B20").

Single Line If…Then…Else Statements

If you are writing a short or simple code, you should use the single-line syntax. If you wish to distinguish between the singly-line and multiple-line syntax, you should look at the block of code that succeeds the Then keyword. If there is nothing succeeding the Then keyword, the block of code is multiple-line. Otherwise, it is a single-line code.

The syntax for Single-line statements is as follows:

```
If condition Then statements Else else_statements
```

These blocks of statements can also be nested in one line by nesting the information within each conditional statement. You can insert the clause Else If in the code, which is similar to the ElseIf clause. You do not need to use the End If keywords in the single-syntax block of code since the program will automatically terminate.

Let us look at some examples[15] where we will use the single-line syntax for the If…Then…Else statements.

If sngMarks > 80 Then MsgBox "Excellent Marks"

If sngMarks > 80 Then MsgBox "Excellent Marks" Else MsgBox "Not Excellent"

'add MsgBox title "Grading":

If sngMarks > 80 Then MsgBox "Excellent Marks", , "Grading"

'using logical operator And in the condition:

If sngMarks > 80 And sngAvg > 80 Then MsgBox "Both Marks & Average are Excellent" Else MsgBox "Not Excellent"

'nesting another If...Then statement:

If sngMarks > 80 Then If sngAvg > 80 Then MsgBox "Both Marks & Average are Excellent"

---

[15] Conditional Statements in Excel VBA - If, Case, For, Do Loops. (2019). Retrieved from https://analysistabs.com/excel-vba/conditional-statements/

Example 1[16]

Sub IfThenSingleLine1()

Dim sngMarks As Single

sngMarks = 85

'Execute multiple statements / codes after Then keyword. Code will return 3 messages: "Excellent Marks - 85 on 90"; "Keep it up!" and "94.44% marks".

If sngMarks = 85 Then MsgBox "Excellent Marks - 85 on 90": MsgBox "Keep it up!": MsgBox Format(85 / 90 * 100, "0.00") & "% marks"

End Sub

Example 2

[17]Sub IfThenSingleLine1()

Dim sngMarks As Single

sngMarks = 85

'Execute multiple statements / codes after Then keyword. Code will return 3 messages: "Excellent Marks - 85 on 90"; "Keep it up!" and "94.44% marks".

---

[16] Conditional Statements in Excel VBA - If, Case, For, Do Loops. (2019). Retrieved from https://analysistabs.com/excel-vba/conditional-statements/

[17] Conditional Statements in Excel VBA - If, Case, For, Do Loops. (2019). Retrieved from https://analysistabs.com/excel-vba/conditional-statements/

If sngMarks = 85 Then MsgBox "Excellent Marks - 85 on 90": MsgBox "Keep it up!": MsgBox Format(85 / 90 * 100, "0.00") & "% marks"

End Sub

Example 3

[18]Sub IfThenSingleLine2()

Dim sngMarks As Single, sngAvg As Single

sngMarks = 85

sngAvg = 75

'nesting If...Then statements. Code will return the message: "Marks are Excellent, but Average is not"

If sngMarks > 80 Then If sngAvg > 80 Then MsgBox "Both Marks & Average are Excellent" Else MsgBox "Marks are Excellent, but Average is not" Else MsgBox "Marks are not Excellent"

End Sub

Example 4

[19]Sub IfThenSingleLine3()

Dim sngMarks As Single

---

[18] Conditional Statements in Excel VBA - If, Case, For, Do Loops. (2019). Retrieved from https://analysistabs.com/excel-vba/conditional-statements/

[19] Conditional Statements in Excel VBA - If, Case, For, Do Loops. (2019). Retrieved from https://analysistabs.com/excel-vba/conditional-statements/

sngMarks = 65

'using the keywords Else If (in single-line syntax), similar to ElseIf (in multiple-line syntax). Procedure will return the message: "Marks are Good".

If sngMarks > 80 Then MsgBox "Marks are Excellent" Else If sngMarks >= 60 Then MsgBox "Marks are Good" Else If sngMarks >= 40 Then MsgBox "Marks are Average" Else MsgBox "Marks are Poor"

End Sub

Select...Case Statement

The Select...Case statement will execute statements or a block of code depending on whether some conditions have been met. It will evaluate an expression and executes one of the many blocks of code depending on what the result is. This statement is similar to the If...The...Else statement.

Syntax

Select Case expression

Case expression_value_1

statements_1

Case expression_value_n

statements_n

Case Else

else_statements

End Select

Expression

This can be a range, field or a variable. The expression can be expressed by using a VBA function -> as "rng.HasFormula" or "IsNumeric(rng)" where the 'rng' is the range variable. The expression can return a String value, Boolean Value, Numeric Value or any other data type. It is important that you specify the expression. It is the value of the expression that the compiler will test and compare with each case in the Select...Case statement. When the values match, the compiler will execute the block of code under the matching Case.

Expression_value

The data type of the expression_value should be the same as the expression or a similar data type. The compiler will compare the value of the expression against the expression_value in each case. If it finds a match, the block of code under the case or the statements will be executed. You must specify at least one expression_value, and the compiler will test the expression against these values in the order they are mentioned in. The expression_values are similar to a list of conditions where the condition must be met for the relevant block of code to be executed.

Statements

The compiler will execute the block of code or statements under a specific case if the value of the expression and the expression_value are the same.

Case Else -> expression_value

When the compiler matches the value of the expression to the expression_value, it will execute the block of code under that case. It will not check the value of the expression against the remaining expression_value. If the compiler does not find a match against any expression_value, it will move to the Case Else clause. The statements under this clause are executed. You do not have to use this clause when you write your code.

Else_statements

As mentioned earlier, the else_statements are included in the Case Else section of the code. If the compiler cannot match the value of the expression to any expression_value, it will execute these statements.

End Select

These keywords[20] terminate the Select…Case block of statements. You must mention these keywords at the end of the Select…Case statements.

Let us look at an example of the Select…Case statements.

Sub selectCase1()

'making strAge equivalent to "young" will return the message "Less than 40 years"

Dim strAge As String

strAge = "young"

Select Case strAge

Case "senior citizen"

MsgBox "Over 60 years"

Case "middle age"

---

[20] Conditional Statements in Excel VBA - If, Case, For, Do Loops. (2019). Retrieved from https://analysistabs.com/excel-vba/conditional-statements/

```
MsgBox "Between 40 to 59 years"

Case "young"

MsgBox "Less than 40 years"

Case Else

MsgBox "Invalid"

End Select

End Sub
```

Using the To Keyword

You can use the To keyword to specify the upper and lower range of all matching values in the expression_value section of the Select...Case statements. The value on the left side of the To keyword should either be less than or equal to the value on the right side of the To keyword. You can also specify the range for a specified set of characters.

Let us look at an example[21].

```
Sub selectCaseTo()

'entering marks as 69 will return the message "Average"; entering marks as 101 will return the message "Out of Range"

Dim iMarks As Integer

iMarks = InputBox("Enter marks")
```

---

[21] Conditional Statements in Excel VBA - If, Case, For, Do Loops. (2019). Retrieved from https://analysistabs.com/excel-vba/conditional-statements/

```
Select Case iMarks

Case 70 To 100

MsgBox "Good"

Case 40 To 69

MsgBox "Average"

Case 0 To 39

MsgBox "Failed"

Case Else

MsgBox "Out of Range"

End Select

End Sub
```

Using the Is Keyword

You can use the Is keyword if you want to include a comparison operator like <>, ==, <=, >=, < or >. If you do not include the Is keyword, the compiler will automatically include it. Let us look at the example[22] below.

```
Sub selectCaseIs()

'if sngTemp equals 39.5, returned message is "Moderately Hot"

Dim sngTemp As Single
```

[22] Conditional Statements in Excel VBA - If, Case, For, Do Loops. (2019). Retrieved from https://analysistabs.com/excel-vba/conditional-statements/

```
sngTemp = 39.5

Select Case sngTemp

Case Is >= 40

MsgBox "Extremely Hot"

Case Is >= 25

MsgBox "Moderately Hot"

Case Is >= 0

MsgBox "Cool Weather"

Case Is < 0

MsgBox "Extremely Cold"

End Select

End Sub
```

Using a comma

You can include multiple ranges or expressions in the Case clause. These ranges and expressions can be separated with a comma. The comma acts like the OR operator. You can also specify multiple expressions and ranges for character strings. Let us look at the example below.

Example 1

```
[23]Sub selectCaseMultiple_1()

'if alpha equates to "Hello", the returned message is "Odd Number or Hello"

Dim alpha As Variant

alpha = "Hello"

Select Case alpha

Case a, e, i, o, u

MsgBox "Vowels"

Case 2, 4, 6, 8

MsgBox "Even Number"

Case 1, 3, 5, 7, 9, "Hello"

MsgBox "Odd Number or Hello"

Case Else

MsgBox "Out of Range"

End Select

End Sub
```

---

[23] Conditional Statements in Excel VBA - If, Case, For, Do Loops. (2019). Retrieved from https://analysistabs.com/excel-vba/conditional-statements/

Example 2

[24]In this example, we are comparing the strings "apples" to "grapes." The compiler will determine the value between "apples" and "grapes" and will use the default comparison method binary.

Sub SelectCaseMultiple_OptionCompare_NotSpecified()

'Option Compare is NOT specified and therefore text comparison will be case-sensitive

'bananas will return the message "Text between apples and grapes, or specifically mangoes, or the numbers 98 or 99"; oranges will return the message "Out of Range"; Apples will return the message "Out of Range".

Dim var As Variant, strResult As String

var = InputBox("Enter")

Select Case var

Case 1 To 10, 11 To 20: strResult = "Number is between 1 and 20"

Case "apples" To "grapes", "mangoes", 98, 99: strResult = "Text between apples and grapes, or specifically mangoes, or the numbers 98 or 99"

Case Else: strResult = "Out of Range"

End Select

MsgBox strResult

End Sub

---

[24] Conditional Statements in Excel VBA - If, Case, For, Do Loops. (2019). Retrieved from https://analysistabs.com/excel-vba/conditional-statements/

Nesting

You can nest the Select...Case block of code or statements within VBA loops, If...Then...Else statements and within a Select...Case block. There is no limit on the number of cases you can include in the code. If you are nesting a Select...Case within another Select...Case, it should be a complete block by itself and also terminate with its End Select.

Example 1

[25]Sub selectCaseNested1()

'check if a range is empty; and if not empty, whether has a numeric value and if numeric then if also has a formula; and if not numeric then what is the text length.

Dim rng As Range, iLength As Integer

Set rng = ActiveSheet.Range("A1")

Select Case IsEmpty(rng)

Case True

MsgBox rng.Address & " is empty"

Case Else

Select Case IsNumeric(rng)

Case True

MsgBox rng.Address & " has a numeric value"

---

[25] Conditional Statements in Excel VBA - If, Case, For, Do Loops. (2019). Retrieved from https://analysistabs.com/excel-vba/conditional-statements/

```
Select Case rng.HasFormula

Case True

MsgBox rng.Address & " also has a formula"

End Select

Case Else

iLength = Len(rng)

MsgBox rng.Address & " has a Text length of " & iLength

End Select

End Select

End Sub
```

Example 2

```
[26]Function StringManipulation(str As String) As String

'This code customizes a string text as follows:

'1. removes numericals from a text string;

'2. removes leading, trailing & inbetween spaces (leaves single space between words);

'3. adds space (if not present) after each exclamation, comma, full stop and question mark;
```

[26] Conditional Statements in Excel VBA - If, Case, For, Do Loops. (2019). Retrieved from https://analysistabs.com/excel-vba/conditional-statements/

'4. capitalizes the very first letter of the string and the first letter of a word after each exclamation, full stop and question mark;

Dim iTxtLen As Integer, iStrLen As Integer, n As Integer, i As Integer, ansiCode As Integer

'--------------------------

'REMOVE NUMERICALS

'chr(48) to chr(57) represent numericals 0 to 9 in ANSI/ASCII character codes

For i = 48 To 57

'remove all numericals from the text string using vba Replace function:

str = Replace(str, Chr(i), "")

Next i

'--------------------------

'REMOVE LEADING, TRAILING & INBETWEEN SPACES (LEAVE SINGLE SPACE BETWEEN WORDS)

'use the worksheet TRIM function. Note: the TRIM function removes space character with ANSI code 32, does not remove the nonbreaking space character with ANSI code 160

str = Application.Trim(str)

'--------------------------

'ADD SPACE (IF NOT PRESENT) AFTER EACH EXCLAMATION, COMMA, DOT AND QUESTION MARK:

'set variable value to string length:

```
iTxtLen = Len(str)

For n = iTxtLen To 1 Step -1

'Chr(32) returns space; Chr(33) returns exclamation; Chr(44) returns comma; Chr(46) returns full stop; Chr(63) returns question mark;

If Mid(str, n, 1) = Chr(33) Or Mid(str, n, 1) = Chr(44) Or Mid(str, n, 1) = Chr(46) Or Mid(str, n, 1) = Chr(63) Then

'check if space is not present:

If Mid(str, n + 1, 1) <> Chr(32) Then

'using Mid & Right functions to add space - note that current string length is used:

str = Mid(str, 1, n) & Chr(32) & Right(str, iTxtLen - n)

'update string length - increments by 1 after adding a space (character):

iTxtLen = iTxtLen + 1

End If

End If

Next n

'---------------------------

'DELETE SPACE (IF PRESENT) BEFORE EACH EXCLAMATION, COMMA, DOT & QUESTION MARK:

'reset variable value to string length:

iTxtLen = Len(str)

For n = iTxtLen To 1 Step -1
```

'Chr(32) returns space; Chr(33) returns exclamation; Chr(44) returns comma; Chr(46) returns full stop; Chr(63) returns question mark;

If Mid(str, n, 1) = Chr(33) Or Mid(str, n, 1) = Chr(44) Or Mid(str, n, 1) = Chr(46) Or Mid(str, n, 1) = Chr(63) Then

'check if space is present:

If Mid(str, n - 1, 1) = Chr(32) Then

'using the worksheet Replace function to delete a space:

str = Application.Replace(str, n - 1, 1, "")

'omit rechecking the same character again - position of n shifts (decreases by 1) due to deleting a space character:

n = n - 1

End If

End If

Next n

'---------------------------

'CAPITALIZE LETTERS:

'capitalize the very first letter of the string and the first letter of a word after each exclamation, full stop and question mark, while all other letters are lowercase

iStrLen = Len(str)

For i = 1 To iStrLen

'determine the ANSI code of each character in the string

ansiCode = Asc(Mid(str, i, 1))

Select Case ansiCode

'97 to 122 are the ANSI codes equating to small cap letters "a" to "z"

Case 97 To 122

If i > 2 Then

'capitalizes a letter whose position is 2 characters after (1 character after, will be the space character added earlier) an exclamation, full stop and question mark:

If Mid(str, i - 2, 1) = Chr(33) Or Mid(str, i - 2, 1) = Chr(46) Or Mid(str, i - 2, 1) = Chr(63) Then

Mid(str, i, 1) = UCase(Mid(str, i, 1))

End If

'capitalize first letter of the string:

ElseIf i = 1 Then

Mid(str, i, 1) = UCase(Mid(str, i, 1))

End If

'if capital letter, skip to next character (ie. next i):

Case Else

GoTo skip

End Select

skip:

Next i

'--------------------------

```
'manipulated string:
StringManipulation = str
End Function
Sub Str_Man()
'specify text string to manipulate & get manipulated string
Dim strText As String
'specify the text string, which is required to be manipulated
strText = ActiveSheet.Range("A1").Value
'the manipulated text string is entered in range A5 of the active sheet, on running the procedure:
ActiveSheet.Range("A5").Value = StringManipulation(strText)
End Sub
```

Go To Statement

You can use the Go To statement to move to a different section of the code or jump a line in the procedure. There are two parts to the Go To statement:

1. The GoTo keywords that are followed by an identifier, also known as the Label.
2. The Label which is followed by a colon and the line of code or a few statements.

If the value of the expression satisfies the condition, the compiler will move to a separate line of code that is indicated in the GoTo statement. You can avoid this statement and use the If…Then…Else statement. The Go To function makes the code unreadable and confusing.

Select...Case Statements Versus the If...Then...Else Statements

The Select...Case and If...Then...Else statements are both conditional statements. In each of these statements either one or more conditions are tested and the compiler will execute the block of code depending on what the result of the evaluation is.

The difference between the two statements is that in the Select...Case statement only one condition is evaluated at a time. The variable that is to be evaluated is initialized or declared in the Select Case expression. The multiple case statements will specify the different values that the variable can take. In the If...Then...Else statement, multiple conditions can be evaluated and the code for different conditions can be executed at the same time.

The Select...Case statement will only test a single variable for several values while the If...Then...Else statement will test multiple variables for different values. In this sense, the If...Then... Else statement is more flexible since you can test multiple variables for different conditions.

If you are testing a large number of conditions, you should avoid using the If...Then...Else statements since they may appear confusing. These statements can also make it difficult for you to read the code.

CHAPTER 7

Working With Strings

A string is an integral part of VBA, and every programmer must work with strings if they want to automate functions in Excel using VBA. There are many manipulations that one can perform on a string including:

- Removing the blanks in a string
- Extracting some parts of a string
- Converting a number into a string
- Finding the characters in a string
- Formatting dates to include weekdays
- Parsing the string into an array
- Comparing different strings

VBA provides you with different functions that you can use to perform these tasks. This chapter will help you understand how you can work with different strings in VBA. This chapter leaves you with some simple examples that you can use for practice.

Points to Remember

You must keep the following points in mind when you want to work with strings.

Original String Does Not Change

When you perform any operation on a string, the original value of the string will never change. VBA will only return a new string with the necessary changes made. If you want to make changes to the original string, you must assign the result of the function to the original string to replace the original string. This concept is covered later in this chapter.

Comparing Two Strings

There are some string functions like Instr() and StrComp() that allow you to include the **Compare** parameter. This parameter works in the following way:

- **vbTextCompare**: The upper and lower case letters in the string are considered the same.
- **vbBinaryCompare**: The upper and lower case letters in the string are treated differently.

Let us look at the following example[27] to see how you can use the Compare parameter in the StrComp() function.

---

[27] String Manipulation in Excel VBA. (2019). Retrieved from https://www.excel-easy.com/vba/string-manipulation.html

```
Sub Comp1()

        ' Prints 0 if the strings do not match

        Debug.Print StrComp("MARoon", "Maroon",
        vbTextCompare)

        ' Prints 1 if the strings do not match

        Debug.Print StrComp("Maroon", "MAROON",
        vbBinaryCompare)

End Sub
```

Instead of using the same parameter every time, you can use the Option Compare. This parameter is defined at the top of any module, and a function that includes the parameter Compare will use this setting as its default. You can use the Option Compare in the following ways:

Option Compare Text

This option makes uses the vbTextCompare as the default compare argument.

Option Compare[28] Text

```
Sub Comp2()

        ' Strings match - uses vbCompareText as Compare argument

        Debug.Print StrComp("ABC", "abc")

        Debug.Print StrComp("DEF", "def")

End Sub
```

[28] String Manipulation in Excel VBA. (2019). Retrieved from https://www.excel-easy.com/vba/string-manipulation.html

Option Compare Binary

This option uses the vbBinaryCompare as the default compare argument.

```
Option Compare[29] Binary

Sub Comp2()

    ' Strings do not match - uses vbCompareBinary as Compare argument

    Debug.Print StrComp("ABC", "abc")

    Debug.Print StrComp("DEF", "def")

End Sub
```

If you do not use the Option Compare statement, VBA uses Option Compare Binary as the default. Please keep these points in mind when we look at the individual string functions.

Appending Strings

You can use the & operator to append strings in VBA. Let us look at some examples of how you can use this operator to append[30] strings.

```
Sub Append()

    Debug.Print "ABC" & "DEF"
```

---

[29] String Manipulation in Excel VBA. (2019). Retrieved from https://www.excel-easy.com/vba/string-manipulation.html

[30] String Manipulation in Excel VBA. (2019). Retrieved from https://www.excel-easy.com/vba/string-manipulation.html

```
        Debug.Print "Jane" & " " & "Smith"

        Debug.Print "Long " & 22

        Debug.Print "Double " & 14.99

        Debug.Print "Date " & #12/12/2015#

End Sub
```

In the example above, there are different types of data that we have converted to string using the quotes. You will see that the plus operator can also be used to append strings in some programs. The difference between using the & operator and + operator is that the latter will only work with string data types. If you use it with any other data type, you will get an error message.

```
        ' You will get the following error:  "Type Mismatch"

        Debug.Print "Long " + 22
```

If you want to use a complex function to append strings, you should use the Format function which is described later in this chapter.

Extracting Parts of a String

In this section, we will look at some functions that you can use to extract information or data from strings.

You can use the Right, Left and Mid functions to extract the necessary parts in a string. These functions[31] are simple to use. The Right function reads the sentence from the right, the Left function reads the

---

[31] String Manipulation in Excel VBA. (2019). Retrieved from https://www.excel-easy.com/vba/string-manipulation.html

sentence from the left and the Mid function will read the sentence from the point that you specify.

```
Sub UseLeftRightMid()

        Dim sCustomer As String

        sCustomer = "John Thomas Smith"

        Debug.Print Left(sCustomer, 4)  ' This will print John

        Debug.Print Right(sCustomer, 5) ' This will print Smith

        Debug.Print Left(sCustomer, 11)  ' This will print John Thomas

        Debug.Print Right(sCustomer, 12)  ' This will print Thomas Smith

        Debug.Print Mid(sCustomer, 1, 4) ' This will print John

        Debug.Print Mid(sCustomer, 6, 6) ' This will print Thomas

        Debug.Print Mid(sCustomer, 13, 5) ' This will print Smith

End Sub
```
[32]

As mentioned earlier, the string functions in VBA do not change the original string but return a new string as the result. In the following example, you will see that the string "FullName" remains unchanged even after the use of the Left function.

---

[32] String Manipulation in Excel VBA. (2019). Retrieved from https://www.excel-easy.com/vba/string-manipulation.html

```
Sub UsingLeftExample()

    Dim Fullname As String

    Fullname = "John Smith"

    Debug.Print "Firstname is: "; Left(Fullname, 4)

    ' The original string remains unchanged

    Debug.Print "Fullname is: "; Fullname

End Sub
```

If you wish to make a change to the original string, you will need to assign the return value of the function to the original string.

```
Sub ChangingString()

    Dim name As String

    name = "John Smith"

    ' The return value of the function is assigned to the original
    string

    name = Left(name, 4)

    Debug.Print "Name is: "; name

End Sub
```

Searching in a String

InStr and InStrRev are two functions that you can use in VBA to search for substrings within a string. If the compiler can find the substring in the string, the position of the string is returned. This position is the index from where the string starts. If the substring is not found, the compiler will return zero. If the original string and substring are null, the value null is returned.

InStr

Description of Parameters

The function is written[33] as follows:

InStr() Start[Optional], String1, String2, Compare[Optional]

1. **Start**: This number specified where the compiler should start looking for the substring within the actual string. The default option is one.
2. **String1**: This is the original string.
3. **String2**: This is the substring that you want the compiler to search for.
4. **Compare**: This is the method we looked at in the first part of this chapter.

The Use and Examples

This function will return the first position in the string where the substring is found. Let us look at the following example:

```
Sub FindSubString()
 Dim name As String
     name = "John Smith"
```

---

[33] String Manipulation in Excel VBA. (2019). Retrieved from https://www.excel-easy.com/vba/string-manipulation.html

' This will return the number 3 which indicates the position of the first h

Debug.Print InStr(name, "h")

' This will return the number 10 which indicates the position of the first h starting from position 4

Debug.Print InStr(4, name, "h")

' This will return 8

Debug.Print InStr(name, "it")

' This will return 6

Debug.Print InStr(name, "Smith")

' This will return zero since the string “SSS” was not found

Debug.Print InStr(name, "SSS")

End Sub

InStrRev

Description of Parameters

The function is written as follows:

InStrRev() StringCheck, StringMatch, Start[Optional], Compare[Optional]

1. **StringCheck**: This is the string that you need to search for.
2. **StringMatch**: This is the string the compiler should look for.
3. **Start**: This number specified where the compiler should start looking for the substring within the actual string. The default option is one.

4. **Compare**: This is the method we looked at in the first part of this chapter.

The Use and Examples

This function is the same as the InStr function except that is starts the search from the end of the original string. You must note that the position that the compiler returns is the position from the start of the sentence. Therefore, if the substring is available only once in the sentence, the InStr() and InStrRev() functions return the same value.

Let us look at some examples[34] of the InStrRev function.

```
Sub UsingInstrRev()

    Dim name As String

    name = "John Smith"

    ' Both functions will return 1 which is the position of the only J

    Debug.Print InStr(name, "J")

    Debug.Print InStrRev(name, "J")

    ' This will return 10 which indicates the second h

    Debug.Print InStrRev(name, "h")

    ' This will return the number 3 and it indicates the first h as searches from position

    Debug.Print InStrRev(name, "h", 9)

    ' This will return 1
```

---

[34] String Manipulation in Excel VBA. (2019). Retrieved from https://www.excel-easy.com/vba/string-manipulation.html

```
Debug.Print InStrRev(name, "John")

End Sub
```

You should use the InStr and InStrRev functions when you want to perform basic searches in strings. If you want to extract some text from a string, the process is slightly complicated.

Removing Blanks

In VBA, you can use the trim functions to remove blanks or spaces either at the start or end of a string.

The Use and Examples

1. [35]**Trim**: Removes the spaces from both the right and left of a string.
2. **LTrim**: Removes the spaces only from the left of the string.
3. **RTrim**: Removes the spaces from the right of the string.

```
Sub TrimStr()

    Dim name As String

    name = "  John Smith  "

    ' Will print "John Smith  "

    Debug.Print LTrim(name)

    ' Will print "  John Smith"

    Debug.Print RTrim(name)
```

[35] String Manipulation in Excel VBA. (2019). Retrieved from https://www.excel-easy.com/vba/string-manipulation.html

```
    ' Will print “John Smith"
    Debug.Print Trim(name)
End Sub
```

Length of a String[36]

You can use Len to return the length of the string. This function will only return the number of characters in the string. You can use different data types if you want to identify the number of bytes in the string.

```
Sub GetLen()
    Dim name As String
    name = "John Smith"
    ' This will print 10
    Debug.Print Len("John Smith")
    ' This will print 3
    Debug.Print Len("ABC")
    ' This will print 4 since the numeric data type Long is 4 bytes in size
    Dim total As Long
    Debug.Print Len(total)
End Sub
```

---

[36] String Manipulation in Excel VBA. (2019). Retrieved from https://www.excel-easy.com/vba/string-manipulation.html

Reversing a String[37]

If you want to reverse the characters in the original string, you can use the StrReverse function. This functions is extremely easy to use.

```
Sub RevStr()

        Dim s As String

        s = "Jane Smith"

        ' This will print htimS enaJ

        Debug.Print StrReverse(s)

End Sub
```

Comparing Strings

You can use the function StrComp to compare two strings.

Description of Parameters

The function is written as follows:

StrComp() String1, String2, Compare[Optional]

1. **String1**: The first string that needs to be compared.
2. **String2**: The second string that needs to be compared.
3. **Compare**: This is the method we looked at in the first part of this chapter.

---

[37] String Manipulation in Excel VBA. (2019). Retrieved from https://www.excel-easy.com/vba/string-manipulation.html

The Use and Examples[38]

Let us look at some examples of how to use the StrComp function:

```
Sub UsingStrComp()

  ' This will return 0

  Debug.Print StrComp("ABC", "ABC", vbTextCompare)

  ' This will return 1

  Debug.Print StrComp("ABCD", "ABC", vbTextCompare)

  ' This will return -1

  Debug.Print StrComp("ABC", "ABCD", vbTextCompare)

  ' This will return Null

  Debug.Print StrComp(Null, "ABCD", vbTextCompare)

End Sub
```

Comparing Strings Using Operators

You can use the equal to sign to compare two strings in VBA. The differences between the equal to sign and the StrComp function are:

- The former will only return true or false
- You cannot combine a Compare parameter with the equal sign since it will only use the Option Compare setting.

---

[38] String Manipulation in Excel VBA. (2019). Retrieved from https://www.excel-easy.com/vba/string-manipulation.html

Let us look at a few examples[39] where we use the equal to sign to compare two strings.

```
Option Compare Text

Sub CompareUsingEquals()

  ' This will return true

        Debug.Print "ABC" = "ABC"

        ' This will return True since the compare text parameter is at the start of the program

        Debug.Print "ABC" = "abc"

        ' This will return false

        Debug.Print "ABCD" = "ABC"

        ' This will return false

        Debug.Print "ABC" = "ABCD"

        ' This will return null

        Debug.Print Null = "ABCD"

End Sub
```

[40]To see if two strings are not equal, you must use the "<>" operator. This operator performs a function that is opposite to the equal to sign.

---

[39] String Manipulation in Excel VBA. (2019). Retrieved from https://www.excel-easy.com/vba/string-manipulation.html

[40] String Manipulation in Excel VBA. (2019). Retrieved from https://www.excel-easy.com/vba/string-manipulation.html

```
Option Compare Text

Sub CompareWithNotEqual()

    ' This will return false

    Debug.Print "ABC" <> "ABC"

    ' This will return false since the Compare Text parameter is at
    the start of the program

    Debug.Print "ABC" <> "abc"

    ' This will return true

    Debug.Print "ABCD" <> "ABC"

    ' This will return true

    Debug.Print "ABC" <> "ABCD"

    ' This will return null

    Debug.Print Null <> "ABCD"

End Sub
```

Comparing Strings Using Pattern Matching

Pattern matching is a technique in VBA that allows you to determine if there is a specific pattern of characters used in a string. For example, there are some times when you will need to check if a specific value has three alphabetic and three numeric characters or if a string is followed by a set of characters or numbers. If the compiler deems that the string follows the specific pattern that you described, it will return “True,” otherwise it will return “False.”

The process of pattern matching is similar to the format function. This means that you can use the pattern matching process in many ways.

In this section, we will look at a few examples which will help you understand how this technique works. Let us take the following string as an example[41]: [abc][!def]]?#X*

Let us look at how this string will work:

1. [abc]: This will represent a character – a, b or c.
2. [!def]: This will represent a character that is not d, e or f.
3. ?: This will represent any character.
4. #: This will represent any digit.
5. X: This represents the character X.
6. *: This means that the string is followed by more characters or zero.

Therefore, this is a valid string.

Now, let us consider the following string: apY6X.

1. a: This character is one of a, b and c.
2. p: This is not a character that is d, e or f.
3. Y: This is any character.
4. 6: This is a digit.
5. X: This is the letter X.

You can now say that the pattern for both strings is the same.

---

[41] String Manipulation in Excel VBA. (2019). Retrieved from https://www.excel-easy.com/vba/string-manipulation.html

Let us look at a code that will show you a variety of results when you use the same pattern:

```
Sub Patterns()

    ' This will print true

    Debug.Print 1; "apY6X" Like "[abc][!def]?#X*"

    ' This will print true since any combination is valid after X

    Debug.Print 2; "apY6Xsf34FAD" Like "[abc][!def]?#X*"

    ' This will print false since the character is not a, b or c

    Debug.Print 3; "dpY6X" Like "[abc][!def]?#X*"

    ' This will print false since the character is one of d, e and f

    Debug.Print 4; "aeY6X" Like "[abc][!def]?#X*"

    ' This will print false since the character at 4 should be a digit.

    Debug.Print 5; "apYAX" Like "[abc][!def]?#X*"

    ' This will print false since the character at position 5 should
    be X.

    Debug.Print 1; "apY6Z" Like "[abc][!def]?#X*"

End Sub
```

Replacing Part of a String

If you want to replace a substring in a string with another string, you should use the replace function. This function will allow you to replace all the instances in a string where the substring is found.

Description of Parameters

The function is written as follows:

Replace() Expression, Find, Replace, Start[Optional], Count[Optional], Compare[Optional]

1. Expression: This is the original string.
2. Find: This is the substring that you want to replace in the Expression string.
3. Replace: This is the substring you want to replace the Find substring with.
4. Start: This is the start position of the string. The position is taken as 1 by default.
5. Count: This is the number of substitutions you want to make. The default is one, which means that all the Find substrings are replaced with the Replace substring.
6. Compare: This is the method we looked at in the first part of this chapter.

The Use and Examples

In the following code, we will look at some examples of how to use the Replace function.

```
Sub ReplaceExamples()

    ' To replace all the question marks in the string with semicolons.

    Debug.Print Replace("A?B?C?D?E", "?", ";")

    ' To replace Smith with Jones
```

```
    Debug.Print Replace("Peter Smith,Ann Smith", "Smith", "Jones")

    ' To replace AX with AB

    Debug.Print Replace("ACD AXC BAX", "AX", "AB")

End Sub
```

The output will be as follows:

A;B;C;D;E

Peter Jones,Sophia Jones

ACD ABC BAB

In the block of code below, we are using the Count optional parameter to determine the number of substitutions you want to make. For example, if you set the parameter equal to one, you are asking the compiler to replace the first occurrence that is found in the 'Find String' section.

```
Sub ReplaceCount()

    ' To replace only the first question mark

    Debug.Print Replace("A?B?C?D?E", "?", ";", Count:=1)

    ' To replace the first two question marks

    Debug.Print Replace("A?B?C?D?E", "?", ";", Count:=2)

End Sub
```

The output will be as follows:

A;B?C?D?E

A;B;C?D?E

If you use the Start optional parameter in the code, you can return only a part of the string. Based on the position that you mention in the Start parameter, the compiler will return the part of the string after that position. When you use this operator, the compiler will ignore the string before the specified start position.

```
Sub ReplacePartial()

    ' This will use the original string from the position 4

    Debug.Print Replace("A?B?C?D?E", "?", ";", Start:=4)

    ' This will use the original string from the position 8

    Debug.Print Replace("AA?B?C?D?E", "?", ";", Start:=8)

    ' There are no items that will be replaced, but it will return the last two values

    Debug.Print Replace("ABCD", "X", "Y", Start:=3)

End Sub
```

The output will be as follows:

```
;C;D;E

;E

CD
```

You may want to replace a lower case or upper case letter in a string, and to do this you can use the Compare parameter. This parameter can be used in different functions. If you want to learn more about this parameter, please read the section above.

```
Sub ReplaceCase()

    ' This will only replace the capitalized A's
```

```
    Debug.Print Replace("AaAa", "A", "X",
    Compare:=vbBinaryCompare)

    ' This will replace all the A's

    Debug.Print Replace("AaAa", "A", "X",
    Compare:=vbTextCompare)

End Sub
```

The output is as follows:

XaXa

XXXX

Multiple Replaces

You can also choose to nest the cells that you would like to replace with more than on string. Let us look at the example[42] below where we will need to replace X and Y with A and B respectively.

```
Sub ReplaceMulti()

    Dim newString As String

    ' Replace the A with X

    newString = Replace("ABCD ABDN", "A", "X")

    ' Replace the B with Y in the new string

    newString = Replace(newString, "B", "Y")
```

---

[42] String Manipulation in Excel VBA. (2019). Retrieved from https://www.excel-easy.com/vba/string-manipulation.html

```
    Debug.Print newString

End Sub
```

In the example below, we will make some changes to the above code to perform this task. The value that is returned after the first function will be used as an argument or it could be used as the string for replacement.

```
Sub ReplaceMultiNested()

    Dim newString As String

    ' To replace A with X and B with Y

    newString = Replace(Replace("ABCD ABDN", "A", "X"), "B", "Y")

    Debug.Print newString

End Sub
```

The result of these replacements will be XYCD XYDN.

CHAPTER 8

Arrays

You can use an array to store multiple items in a single container or variable, and use that container in your program. An array is analogous to a large box with a finite or infinite number of smaller boxes inside it. Each box will store a value depending on the data type of the array. You can also choose the number of small boxes you want to store data in. Remember that you can use an array only when you want to store items that have the same data type.

Structured Storage

An array is a list of items that have the same data type. One example of an array can be a to-do list that you prepare. The paper that contains the list of your tasks will form the single container, and this container holds numerous strings, and every string will list the tasks that you need to perform. You can also create the same paper in VBA using an array. An array can be defined using numerous techniques, and each of these techniques will use a similar approach.

Example

[43]‘ Tell VBA to start all arrays at 0.

Option Base 0

Public Sub SingleDimension()

‘ Define an output string.

Dim Output As String

‘ Define a variant to hold individual strings.

Dim IndividualString As Variant

‘ Define the array of strings.

Dim StringArray(5) As String

‘ Fill each array element with information.

StringArray(0) = “This”

StringArray(1) = “Is”

StringArray(2) = “An”

StringArray(3) = “Array”

StringArray(4) = “Of”

StringArray(5) = “Strings”

‘ Use the For Each...Next statement to get each array

---

[43] Kelly, P. (2019). The Complete Guide to Using Arrays in Excel VBA - Excel Macro Mastery. Retrieved from https://excelmacromastery.com/excel-vba-array/

```
' element and place it in a string.
For Each IndividualString In StringArray
' Create a single output string with the array
' array elements.
Output = Output + IndividualString + " "
Next
' Display the result.
MsgBox Trim(Output), _
vbInformation Or vbOKOnly, _
"Array Content"
End Sub
```

If you look at the code above, you will notice that it starts with the statement "Option Base 0." This statement will let VBA know that it should count the elements in the array starting with zero. The default setting is that VBA will count the elements in the array from zero. Most programming languages use zero as the starting point, and it is for this reason that the default for VBA is zero. Most of the older versions of VBA begin counting the elements in the array using 1 as the starting point.

If you want to use the code that you write in different environments, you should always include the Option Base statement. Since an array always starts at zero, and not one, you can store six elements although you define that the array should have five elements. The number that you include in the declaration does not define the number of elements in the array.

Array Types

An array can be classified into different types and this can be done using different methods. An array can be classified into different types depending on the data type of the elements in the array. An integer array is very different from a string array, and you can be certain that the elements in the array are distinct. You can use the Variant data type if you want to mix the data types in the array. Ensure that you are careful about using this data type since it can lead to some errors which will can be difficult for you to debug.

You can also define dimensions in an array which will define the directions in which the array can be allowed to hold any information. You can have a single-dimensional array, a two-dimensional array or an n-dimensional array, where n stands for a number.

Example: Adding an Element to an Array

```
Dim a As Range

Dim arr As Variant  'Just a Variant variable (i.e. don't pre-define it as an array)

For Each a In Range.Cells

        If IsEmpty(arr) Then

        arr = Array(a.value) 'Make the Variant an array with a single element

        Else

        ReDim Preserve arr(UBound(arr) + 1) 'Add next array element

        arr(UBound(arr)) = a.value     'Assign the array element

        End If

Next
```

VBA Array

In this section, we will look at the steps you need to follow to create an array.

Step 1 – Create A New Workbook

1. Open Microsoft Excel.

2. Save the excel workbook with the extension .xlsm

Step 2 – Add A Command Button

Now that you are familiar with creating an interface in a workbook. The previous chapters in the book will help you gather more information about the subroutines or subs and functions in VBA.

1. Add a command button to the active worksheet.

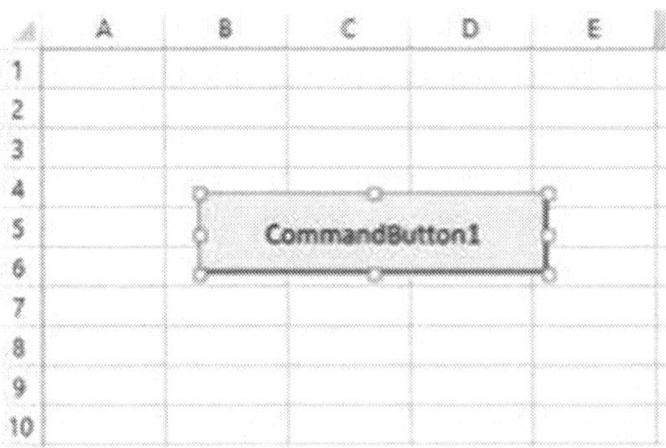

2. Set the property name to cmdLoadBeverages.

3. Now, set the Caption Property as Load Beverages.

The interface should now display the following:

Step 3 – Save The File

1. Now, save the file in the macro-enabled form of Excel.

Step 4 – Write The Code

The next step is to write the code for the application that you have developed:

1. You can view the code by right-clicking on the button.

2. Now, add the code below in the code window.

```
Private Sub cmdLoadBeverages_Click()

        Dim Drinks(1 To 4) As String

        Drinks(1) = "Pepsi"

        Drinks(2) = "Coke"

        Drinks(3) = "Fanta"

        Drinks(4) = "Juice"

        Sheet1.Cells(1, 1).Value = "My Favorite Beverages"

        Sheet1.Cells(2, 1).Value = Drinks(1)

        Sheet1.Cells(3, 1).Value = Drinks(2)

        Sheet1.Cells(4, 1).Value = Drinks(3)

        Sheet1.Cells(5, 1).Value = Drinks(4)

End Sub
```

Example To Enter Student Marks

Without An Array

In the example below, we will look at how you can enter the marks for every student without using an array.

```
Public Sub StudentMarks()

    With ThisWorkbook.Worksheets("Sheet1")

    ' Declare variable for each student

    Dim Student1 As Integer

    Dim Student2 As Integer

    Dim Student3 As Integer

    Dim Student4 As Integer

    Dim Student5 As Integer

    ' Read student marks from cell

    Student1 = .Range("C2").Offset(1)

    Student2 = .Range("C2").Offset(2)

    Student3 = .Range("C2").Offset(3)

    Student4 = .Range("C2").Offset(4)

    Student5 = .Range("C2").Offset(5)

    ' Print student marks

    Debug.Print "Students Marks"

    Debug.Print Student1

    Debug.Print Student2

    Debug.Print Student3

    Debug.Print Student4

    Debug.Print Student5

    End With

End Sub
```

The output will be the following,

Using An Array

```
Public Sub StudentMarksArr()

    With ThisWorkbook.Worksheets("Sheet1")

    ' Declare an array to hold marks for 5 students

    Dim Students(1 To 5) As Integer

    ' Read student marks from cells C3:C7 into array

    Dim i As Integer

    For i = 1 To 5

    Students(i) = .Range("C2").Offset(i)

    Next i

    ' Print student marks from the array

    Debug.Print "Students Marks"

    For i = LBound(Students) To UBound(Students)

    Debug.Print Students(i)

    Next i

    End With

End Sub
```

Notice the difference in the variables used in the two programs, and also notice the length of the program.

Example With Loops

[44]Public Sub ArrayLoops()

```
    ' Declare  array

    Dim arrMarks(0 To 5) As Long

    ' Fill the array with random numbers

    Dim i As Long

    For i = LBound(arrMarks) To UBound(arrMarks)

    arrMarks(i) = 5 * Rnd

    Next i

    ' Print out the values in the array

    Debug.Print "Location", "Value"

    For i = LBound(arrMarks) To UBound(arrMarks)

    Debug.Print i, arrMarks(i)

    Next i

End Sub
```

---

[44] Kelly, P. (2019). The Complete Guide to Using Arrays in Excel VBA - Excel Macro Mastery. Retrieved from https://excelmacromastery.com/excel-vba-array/

Sorting An Array

```
Sub QuickSort(arr As Variant, first As Long, last As Long)
 Dim vCentreVal As Variant, vTemp As Variant
 Dim lTempLow As Long
 Dim lTempHi As Long
 lTempLow = first
 lTempHi = last
 vCentreVal = arr((first + last) \ 2)
 Do While lTempLow <= lTempHi
        Do While arr(lTempLow) < vCentreVal And lTempLow < last
        lTempLow = lTempLow + 1
        Loop
        Do While vCentreVal < arr(lTempHi) And lTempHi > first
        lTempHi = lTempHi - 1
        Loop
        If lTempLow <= lTempHi Then
        ' Swap values
        vTemp = arr(lTempLow)
        arr(lTempLow) = arr(lTempHi)
        arr(lTempHi) = vTemp
        ' Move to next positions
```

```
        lTempLow = lTempLow + 1
        lTempHi = lTempHi - 1
        End If
        Loop
        If first < lTempHi Then QuickSort arr, first, lTempHi
If lTempLow < last Then QuickSort arr, lTempLow, last
End Sub
```

Example For Creating A Two-Dimensional Array

[45]
```
Public Sub TwoDimArray()
        ' Declare a two dimensional array
        Dim arrMarks(0 To 3, 0 To 2) As String
        ' Fill the array with text made up of i and j values
        Dim i As Long, j As Long
        For i = LBound(arrMarks) To UBound(arrMarks)
        For j = LBound(arrMarks, 2) To UBound(arrMarks, 2)
        arrMarks(i, j) = CStr(i) & ":" & CStr(j)
        Next j
        Next i
```

---

[45] Kelly, P. (2019). The Complete Guide to Using Arrays in Excel VBA - Excel Macro Mastery. Retrieved from https://excelmacromastery.com/excel-vba-array/

```
' Print the values in the array to the Immediate Window
Debug.Print "i", "j", "Value"
For i = LBound(arrMarks) To UBound(arrMarks)
For j = LBound(arrMarks, 2) To UBound(arrMarks, 2)
Debug.Print i, j, arrMarks(i, j)
Next j
Next i
End Sub
```

CHAPTER 9

Error Handling And Debugging

Error handling is a common practice that every programmer uses to anticipate any error conditions that may arise when the program is run, and also include a few statements in the code. There are three types of errors that one can come across: run time errors that occur when the VBA editor cannot execute a specific statement in the code; compiler errors where a required variable has not been detected; and user entry data errors where the user does not enter the right type of information. This chapter will focus on run time errors since those errors are difficult to solve. The other two types are easy for the user to identify and correct. One of the most typical run time errors includes the one where the VBA editor is trying to access a workbook or worksheet that does not exist or is dividing a number by zero. The example being used in this chapter is trying to divide a number by zero.

It is important to include as many checks as possible when you write a program since that will help you ensure that there will be no run time errors when you write the code. This means that you should always ensure that every workbook or worksheet that you refer to in your code is present. You must also ensure that you are using the right name. When you check the application while writing the code, you can ensure that you avoid these silly mistakes. It is always good to detect the error while writing the code, and not when the application runs.

If you have written the code well, but still get a run time error and do not have any code written to handle those errors, VBA will display the error in a dialog box. When you are still building the application, you can welcome these errors. You cannot, however, be okay with receiving these errors when the application is being tested or is in the production environment. An error handling code will identify the error and correct that error immediately. The goal behind including an error handling code is to prevent the occurrence of any unhandled errors.

In this chapter, we will refer to the Property Procedure, Function and Sub as procedures and Exit Function, Exit Sub and Exit Property as an exit statement. End Function, End Sub, End and End Property will be represented by the words 'end statement.'

The On Error Statement

The On Error statement is at the heart of an error handling process. If a run time error occurs, this statement will instruct VBA to ignore the error and move on. There are three forms for the On Error statement:

1. On Error Goto 0
2. On Error Resume Next
3. On Error Goto <label>:

On Error Goto 0 is the default in VBA. This statement will indicate to VBA that it should always display the run time error in a dialog box if there is an error in the program. This will give you a chance to enter the debug mode and check the code. You can also choose to terminate the code. The On Error Goto 0 is the same as not including an error handling statement in your code. The error will prompt VBA to display the standard window.

The On Error Resume Next is one statement that most programmers misuse. This statement will instruct VBA to ignore the line of code with the error and move to the next line. Remember that this does not fix your code in any way, but will only tell VBA to act as if there was no error in the code. This will have a negative effect on the code. Therefore, it is important that you test your code for any errors and then fix them using appropriate methods. For the code below, you can fix the error by executing the program depending on whether the value of the variable Err.Number is zero or not.

```
On Error Resume Next

N = 1 / 0        ' cause an error

If Err.Number <> 0 Then

N = 1

End If
```

In the code above, the value 1/0 is being assigned to the variable N. This approach is incorrect since VBA will give you the Division by Zero Error (Error 11). Since you have the On Error Resume Next statement, the code will continue to run. The statement will then assign a different value to the variable N once it tests the value for Err.Number.

The third form is the On Error Goto <label>. This line will let VBA know that it will need to execute a specific line of code or the line of code that is present immediately after a specific line label when an error occurs. Once the error occurs, VBA will ignore all the code between the specified line label and the error line.

```
On Error Goto ErrHandler:
```

```
N = 1 / 0        ' cause an error
'
' more code
'
Exit Sub
ErrHandler:
' error handling code
Resume Next
End Sub
```

Enabled And Active Error Handlers

VBA will create an error handler when the On Error statement is executed. You must remember that VBA can only activate the error handler block of code at a specific point, and behave according to the comments given in that block. If there are any errors, VBA will execute the code in the error handler block. Based on the On Error Goto <label> statement, VBA will execute the code provided in that location. The error handler block of code should either fix the error in the program or resume the execution of the main program. The error handler can also be used to terminate the program. You should not use it to skip a few lines of code. For instance, the code below will not function correctly:

```
    On Error GoTo Err1:
    Debug.Print 1 / 0
    ' more code
Err1:
```

```
On Error GoTo Err2:

Debug.Print 1 / 0

' more code
```

When the first error occurs, the execution of the code will be transferred to the block of code under Err1. The On Error statement will not identify the error since the error handler is active when the next error comes.

The Resume Statement

You can use the Resume statement to let VBA know that it should resume the execution of any code at a specific point or line in the code. Remember that you can use this statement only when you have an error handling code block. Do not use the Goto statement to tell VBA where it needs to go to execute the error handling code since this will lead to some issues.

There are three syntactic forms that the Resume statement takes:

1. Resume
2. Resume Next
3. Resume <label>

When you use the first form of the Resume statement, you will be instructing VBA to resume the execution of the program from the line that has the code. When you do this, you should ensure that the error handling code can fix the issue. Otherwise, the code will enter a loop since it will constantly jump between the line that has the error and the error handling code. In the example below, we will try to activate a worksheet that does not exist. You will receive the following error when you do this: "Subscript Out of Range." The compiler will then jump to the error handling code, and this code will create a sheet that will solve the problem.

```
On Error GoTo ErrHandler:

Worksheets("NewSheet").Activate

Exit Sub

ErrHandler:

If Err.Number = 9 Then

' sheet does not exist, so create it

Worksheets.Add.Name = "NewSheet"

' go back to the line of code that caused the problem

Resume

End If
```

The second form of the Resume method is Resume Next. This statement will let VBA know that it should execute the line of code that comes immediately after the line that gave rise to the error. The code below will set a value to the variable N, and this gives rise to an error. The error handling code will then assign the value 1 to the variable which will allow VBA to execute the rest of the program.

```
On Error GoTo ErrHandler:

N = 1 / 0

Debug.Print N

Exit Sub

ErrHandler:
```

```
N = 1

' Move to the line that is immediately after the error

Resume Next
```

The third form of the Resume statement is Resume <label> form. This type of similar to the On Error Goto <label> statement. The former statement will tell VBA to execute the program from the line label. This means that it will avoid looking at the section of the code where there is an error. For example,

```
On Error GoTo ErrHandler:

N = 1 / 0

'

' This section contains the block of statements that will be skipped if there is an error

'

Label1:

'

' more code to execute

'

Exit Sub

ErrHandler:

' go back to the line at Label1:

Resume Label1:
```

An error object can either be reset or cleared using any form of the Resume statement.

Error Handling With Multiple Procedures

There is no need to include the error code in all procedures. VBA will always use the last On Error statement and act accordingly if there is any error in the program. The error is handled in the method mentioned above if the code causing the error is present in the same procedure as the last On Error statement. If there is no error handling code in the program, VBA will work backward and reach the incorrect section in the code. For example, a procedure A calls B and B calls C, and only procedure A has an error handling code. If an error occurs in C, VBA will go back to the error handling code in procedure A. It will skip all the code in procedure B.

A Note Of Caution

When you deal with errors, you may want to use the On Error Resume Next statement. This is a bad way to build a program since it is essential that you solve any error that you may come across. You must remember that this statement does not skip an error, but ignores it.

CHAPTER 10

How To Improve The Performance Of Macros

There are times when VBA will run very slowly, and this is certainly frustrating. The good news is that there are some steps that you can take to improve the performance of the macro. This chapter will provide some information on the different steps you should take to improve the speed and performance of a macro. Regardless of whether you are an IT administrator, end user or a developer, you can use these tips to your benefit.

Close Everything Except For The VBA Essentials

The first thing to do to improve the performance of VBA is to turn off all the unnecessary features like screen updating, animation, automatic events and calculations when the macro runs. All these features will always add an extra overhead which will slow the macro down. This always happens when the macro needs to modify or change many cells and trigger a lot of recalculations or screen updates.

The code below will show you how you can enable or disable the following:

- Animations
- Screen updates
- Manual Calculations

```
Option Explicit

Dim lCalcSave As Long

Dim bScreenUpdate As Boolean

Sub SwitchOff(bSwitchOff As Boolean)

 Dim ws As Worksheet

 With Application

        If bSwitchOff Then

        ' OFF

        lCalcSave = .Calculation

        bScreenUpdate = .ScreenUpdating

        .Calculation = xlCalculationManual

        .ScreenUpdating = False

        .EnableAnimations = False

        '

        ' switch off display pagebreaks for all worksheets

        '
```

```
        For Each ws In ActiveWorkbook.Worksheets

        ws.DisplayPageBreaks = False

        Next ws

        Else

        ' ON

        If .Calculation <> lCalcSave And lCalcSave <> 0 Then
        .Calculation = lCalcSave

        .ScreenUpdating = bScreenUpdate

        .EnableAnimations = True

   End If

  End With

End Sub

Sub Main()

  SwitchOff(True) ' turn off these features

  MyFunction() ' do your processing here

  SwitchOff(False) ' turn these features back on

End Sub
```

Disabling All The Animations Using System Settings

You can disable animations through the Ease of Access center in Windows. You can use this center to disable some specific features in Excel by going to the Ease of Access or Advanced Tabs on the menu. For more information, please use the following link:

https://support.office.com/en-us/article/turn-off-office-animations-9ee5c4d2-d144-4fd2-b670-22cef9fa

Disabling Office Animations Using Registry Settings

You can always disable office animations on different computers by changing the appropriate registry key using a group policy setting.

HIVE: HKEY_CURRENT_USER

Key Path: Software\Microsoft\Office\16.0\Common\Graphics

Key Name: DisableAnimations

Value type: REG_DWORD

Value data: 0x00000001 (1)

If you use the Registry Editor incorrectly, you can cause some serious problems across the system. You may need to reinstall Windows to use the editor correctly. Microsoft will help you solve the problems of a Registry Editor, but you should use this tool if you are willing to take the risk.

Removing Unnecessary Selects

Most people use the select method in the VBA code, but they add it in places where it is not necessary to use them. This keyword will trigger some cell events like conditional formatting and animations which will hinder the performance of the macro. If you remove all the unnecessary selects, you can improve the performance of the macro. The following example will show you the code before and after you make a change to remove all the extra selects.

Before

```
Sheets("Order Details").Select

Columns("AC:AH").Select

Selection.ClearContents
```

After

```
Sheets("Order Details").Columns("AC:AH").ClearContents
```

Using The With Statement To Read Object Properties

When you work with objects, you should the With statement to decrease the number of times that the compiler reads the properties of the object. In the example below, see how the code changes when you use the With statement.

Before

```
Range("A1").Value = “Hello”

Range("A1").Font.Name = “Calibri”

Range("A1").Font.Bold = True

Range("A1").HorizontalAlignment = xlCenter
```

After

```
With Range("A1")

  .Value2 = “Hello”

  .HorizontalAlignment = xlCenter

          With .Font

          .Name = “Calibri”
```

```
        .Bold = True
        End With
End With
```

Using Arrays And Ranges

It is expensive to read and write to cells every time in Excel using VBA. You incur an overhead every time there is some movement of data between Excel and VBA. This means that you should always reduce the number of times the data moves between Excel and VBA. It is at such a time that ranges are useful. Instead of writing or reading the data individually to every cell within a loop, you can simply read the entire range into an array, and use that array in the loop. The example below will show you how you can use a range to read and write the values at once without having to read each cell individually.

```
Dim vArray As Variant
Dim iRow As Integer
Dim iCol As Integer
Dim dValue As Double
vArray = Range("A1:C10000").Value2 ‘ read all the values at once from the Excel cells, put into an array
For iRow = LBound(vArray, 1) To UBound(vArray, 1)
 For iCol = LBound(vArray, 2) To UBound(vArray, 2)
        dValue = vArray (iRow, iCol)
        If dValue > 0 Then
        dValue=dValue*dValue ‘ Change the values in the array, not the cells
```

```
        vArray(iRow, iCol) = dValue
    End If
Next iCol
Next iRow
Range("A1:C10000").Value2 = vArray ' writes all the results back to the range at once
```

Use .Value2 Instead Of .Text or .Value

You can retrieve your values in different ways from a cell. The property you use to retrieve that information will have an impact on the performance of your code.

.Text

This is the most common property used to retrieve information from a cell. This will return a formatted value in the cell. It is complicated to only retrieve the formatted value of a cell and not just its value. It is for this reason that .Text is slow.

.Value

This keyword is an improvement over the .Text since this only retrieves the value and not the format of that value from the cell. If a cell is formatted as a currency or date, the .Value keyword will only return the VBA currency of VBA date which will truncate at decimal places.

.Value2

.Value2 on returns the underlying value of the cell. This function does not use any formatting and is faster than both the .Text and .Value keywords. It works faster than the previous keywords when it comes to working with numbers, and is faster if you are using a variant array.

To learn more about these keywords, you should read the following blog post: https://fastexcel.wordpress.com/2011/11/30/text-vs-value-vs-value2-slow-text-and-how-to-avoid-it/

Avoid Using Copy And Paste

If you use a Macro Recorder to record the operations that also include copy and paste, the code will use these methods as a default operation. It is easier to avoid using the copy and paste method in VBA, and use some internal operations alone to perform those operations. It is easier to copy information faster if you only copy the values and not the formatting. You can also use these internal operations to copy the formulae. The following example will show you how you can avoid using the copy and paste options.

Before

```
Range("A1").Select

Selection.Copy

Range("A2").Select

ActiveSheet.Paste
```

After

```
' Approach 1: copy everything (formulas, values and formatting

Range("A1").Copy Destination:=Range("A2")

' Approach 2: copy values only

Range("A2").Value2 = Range("A1").Value2

' Approach 3: copy formulas only

Range("A2").Formula = Range("A1").Formula
```

If you think that the code is still functioning slowly, you can use the following fix: https://support.microsoft.com/en-in/help/2817672/macro-takes-longer-than-expected-to-execute-many-in

Use The Option Explicit Keyword To Catch Undeclared Variables

Option Explicit is one of the many Module directives that you can use in VBA. This directive will instruct VBA about how it should treat a code within a specific module. If you use Option Explicit, you should ensure that all the variables in the code are declared. If there is any variable that is not declared, it will throw a compile error. This will help you catch any variables that have been named incorrectly. It will also help to improve the performance of the macro where variables are defined at different times. You can set this by typing "Option Explicit" at the top of every module you write. Alternatively, you can check the "Require Variable Declaration" in the VBA editor under "Tools -> Options."

CHAPTER 11

How to Redirect the Flow

Using the GoTo Statement Correctly

The GoTo statement will allow you to redirect the flow of the program. Ensure that you understand how you can redirect the flow of the program, and see if there are different alternatives like using a loop. If you do not think there is any other way to do it, you can use the GoTo statement.

There are times when you will run into a situation where an existing program flow stops working, and you will need to disrupt it and move the compiler to another section of the code. This is where you can use the GoTo statement since it allows you to redirect the flow of the program. If you use this statement carefully, you can overcome different programming problems. That being said, the GoTo statement does lead to many other problems as well since it can be misused by the programmer. An amateur will want to use the GoTo statement since that will help them overlook programming errors. This means that they will begin to avoid fixing errors. Remember to use to GoTo statement with extreme care, and design the flow of your code well. You should also try to fix the errors in the code while writing it.

Loops

Never use the GoTo statement if you want to replace the end statement in a loop. The statements in the loop will always give the statements outside the loop an input value. Additionally, a standard loop statement always has the necessary keywords that will ensure that there are minimal or no errors.

Exits

You should always use the End statement instead of the GoTo statement if you want to exit a program.

Program Flow Problems

If there is any problem in the flow of the program that you have written, you must check the pseudo-code and then design the code again. This will help you ensure that the design for your code is correct. You may also need to change the design if necessary. Never make the assumption that the design is always correct, especially if you are doing this for the first time.

CHAPTER 12

Working with Excel Workbooks and Worksheets

The Workbook Collection

If you want to know the different workbooks you have open at a specific time, you can use the Workbooks Collection. You can also select the one workbook that you want to include in your program. This workbook is now a workbook object, and it provides all the general information about the file. You can use this object to access other objects in that document like Worksheet objects and Chart objects.

Example:

```
Public Sub WorkbookDemo()

' Holds the output data.

Dim Output As String

' Get the test workbook.

Dim ActiveWorkbook As Workbook

Set ActiveWorkbook =
```

```
Application.Workbooks("ExcelObjects.xls")
' Get the workbook name and location.
Output = "Name: " + ActiveWorkbook.Name + vbCrLf + _
"Full Name: " + ActiveWorkbook.FullName + vbCrLf + _
"Path: " + ActiveWorkbook.Path + vbCrLf + vbCrLf
' Holds the current sheet.
Dim CurrSheet As Worksheet
' Look for every sheet.
Output = "Worksheet List:" + vbCrLf
For Each CurrSheet In ActiveWorkbook.Worksheets
Output = Output + CurrSheet.Name + vbCrLf
Next
' Holds the current chart.
Dim CurrChart As Chart
' Look for every chart.
Output = Output + vbCrLf + "Chart List:" + vbCrLf
For Each CurrChart In ActiveWorkbook.Charts
Output = Output + CurrChart.Name + vbCrLf
Next
' Display the output.
MsgBox Output, vbInformation Or vbOKOnly, "Object List"
End Sub
```

The code begins by using the Application.Workbooks collection that will allow you to look at the different Workbook objects that you have open. You can also use it to retrieve one workbook object. Ensure that you use the correct name of the workbook that you want to open, and also include the extension of the file that you are trying to retrieve. The resulting workbook object will contain all that information about that document. This object will also provide some summary information about the document, and you can use that information to control and maintain the window. You can also add new elements or objects like worksheets to the workbook.

Once the workbook is accessed, the VBA compiler will use the ActiveWorkbook object to access the different worksheet objects that are present in the list. The code will always rely on the For Each… Next statement to access the different worksheet objects. You can also use an index if you want to access individual worksheets. The Active Worksheet will contain all the necessary methods and properties that you can use to manipulate the data in the worksheet, including embedded objects like pictures and charts. All the worksheets in the workbook will appear in the ActiveWorkbook object list by their object name. This will allow you to access them without using the Worksheet collection.

When you use the ActiveWorkbook object, you can only view the independent chart objects. You can also access any Chart object in the worksheet using the same technique that you use to access a worksheet object. The only difference here is that you cannot use the Worksheets collection, but will need to use the Charts collection. Ensure that the chart names will always appear in the object list when you look at the objects in the Active Workbook. This means that you do not need to use the Charts collection to access a chart.

The Worksheet Collection

One of the best ways to access any worksheet regardless of the situation is to use the Sheets collection. You should not follow the hierarchy of Excel objects if you want to identify the worksheet that you want to work with. If you access the worksheet that is at the top of the pyramid, it will mean that there are no objects that exist at the lower levels of the pyramid. Therefore, this technique can be looked at as a tradeoff.

You can always access any sheet type, and not only the worksheet that you will be using if you are using the Sheets collection. Any object, including a standalone Chart object, will also be a part of the worksheet. In the previous example, you will notice that the worksheet and chart objects are treated as separate objects.

Example:

```
Public Sub ListSheets()

‘ An individual entry.

Dim ThisEntry As Variant

‘ Holds the output data.

Dim Output As String

‘ Get the current number of worksheets.

Output = “Sheet Count: “ + _

CStr(Application.Sheets.Count)

‘ List each worksheet in turn.

For Each ThisEntry In Application.Sheets

‘ Verify there is a sheet to work with.
```

```
If ThisEntry.Type = XlSheetType.xlWorksheet Then

Output = Output + vbCrLf + ThisEntry.Name

End If

Next

‘ Display the result.

MsgBox Output, _

vbInformation or vbOKOnly, _

“Worksheet List”

End Sub
```

In the above example, we are creating a Variant data type that will hold different types of sheets. If you use a Worksheet or Chart object, the code that you write will fail since you will not receive the type that you are looking for, although the type returned is valid. The issue with using the Variant data type is that the editor in VBA will not provide balloon help or automatic completion. You must ensure that the method you want to use is typed in correctly, and you always use the correct property names.

Once the necessary variables are all created, you will see the number of worksheets present in the workbook. Remember that this number not only includes the worksheets in the workbook, but also includes the charts in that workbook.

The For Each… Next Loop will retrieve every sheet in turn. You should also notice how the If… Then statement is being used to compare the values of the XlSheetType.xlWorksheet constant and the Variant data type. You can always separate a worksheet that you are using from the other objects in the Sheets collection type if necessary.

Charts Collection

You can use the Charts collection to design or build a custom chart if necessary. One of the advantages of creating a chart using a code is that it will not use too much space, and you can spend very little time when it comes to creating numerous charts.

Example:

```
Public Sub BuildChart()

‘ Create a new chart.

Dim NewChart As Chart

Set NewChart = Charts.Add(After:=Charts(Charts.Count))

‘ Change the name.

NewChart.Name = “Added Chart”

‘ Create a series for the chart.

Dim TheSeries As Series

NewChart.SeriesCollection.Add _

Source:=Worksheets(“My Data Sheet”).Range(“A$3:B$8”)

Set TheSeries = NewChart.SeriesCollection(1)

‘ Change the chart type.

TheSeries.ChartType = xl3DPie

‘ Change the series title.

TheSeries.Name = “Data from My Data Sheet”

‘ Perform some data formatting.
```

```
With TheSeries
.HasDataLabels = True
.DataLabels.ShowValue = True
.DataLabels.Font.Italic = True
.DataLabels.Font.Size = 14
End With
' Modify the chart's legend.
With NewChart
.HasLegend = True
.Legend.Font.Size = 14
End With
' Modify the 3-D view.
With NewChart
.Pie3DGroup.FirstSliceAngle = 90
.Elevation = 45
End With
' Format the chart title.
NewChart.ChartTitle.Font.Bold = True
NewChart.ChartTitle.Font.Size = 18
NewChart.ChartTitle.Format.Line.DashStyle _
= msoLineSolid
```

```
NewChart.ChartTitle.Format.Line.Style = msoLineSingle

NewChart.ChartTitle.Format.Line.Weight = 2

‘ Compute the optimal plot area size.

Dim Size As Integer

If NewChart.PlotArea.Height > NewChart.PlotArea.Width

Then

Size = NewChart.PlotArea.Width

Else

Size = NewChart.PlotArea.Height

End If

‘ Reduce the plot area by 10%.

Size = Size - (Size * 0.1)

‘ Format the plot area.

With NewChart.PlotArea

.Interior.Color = RGB(255, 255, 255)

.Border.LineStyle = XlLineStyle.xlLineStyleNone

.Height = Size

.Width = Size

.Top = 75

.Left = 100

End With
```

```
' Format the labels.

Dim ChartLabels As DataLabel

Set ChartLabels = TheSeries.DataLabels(0)

ChartLabels.Position = xlLabelPositionOutsideEnd

End Sub
```

In the example above, you are instructing VBA to create a new chart. This chart will be the last chart in the workbook, but is not the last item in the workbook. This means that if a worksheet is created after the last chart, it will still appear in the object list. The NewChart.Name property will allow you to change the name that will appear at the bottom of the chart. This property will not change the name of the chart.

The chart is blank at this point, and you should add at least one of the series to the chart if you want to display any data on it. Remember that a pie chart can only display the data for one series at a time, but you can use different charts if you want to show multiple data series. For instance, you can show multiple data series using a bubble chart. In the next part of the data, you will create a data series using the information present in the worksheet "My Data Sheet." You will notice that the code will set the TheSeries variable equal to the output. Therefore, you must include an additional step that will help you obtain the new series from the Series Collection.

There are two columns that hold information in the Range property. If you are using Excel 2007 and above, the first column is used to define the XValues property in the chart. This property is used to determine the different entries in the legend for a pie chart. These values will appear at the bottom if you are using a Bar chart. In both the pie chart and the bar chart, you should display the labels on the screen. This will help you see their effect on the display area.

CHAPTER 13

Some Problems With Spreadsheets And How To Overcome Them

Most people use Excel to make a repository. This is because it is easy to make a list of small items for yourself or your colleagues in Excel. You may perhaps want to use some formulae to create something sophisticated. You may also want to use macros to automate the process of collecting and processing data. You can do this by typing an equal to sign in the cell before you write the formula. Excel will be your guide. There are some problems that everybody will face when it comes to using Excel, and that is its simplicity. You may start with a small project in Excel, and this project will grow until it becomes a daunting task. At this point, you may also face some issues with stability and speed, or some development problem that you cannot solve.

This chapter examines some of the common issues that people come across when they use spreadsheets, and also provides some solutions to tackle those problems. It will also tell you when you should switch to a database instead of sticking to Excel.

Multi-User Editing

When an Excel system begins to grow, you will quickly run into a problem where only one user can open the workbook at a time and make changes to it. Any other person who wants to open the workbook will be notified that someone already has the book open and that they can view the workbook as a read-only version or wait until the file is closed by the first user. Excel does promise to let you know when the first user has closed the file, but this is a hollow promise since Excel does not always check the status, and there are times when it may never give you an update. Even if it does give you an update, someone may already have opened the file before you.

You can get around this in the following ways:

- You should use Excel Online. This application is a web-based and abridged version of Microsoft Excel.
- Turn on the feature that will allow you to share the workbook.
- Split the workbook into smaller workbooks. This will allow different users to access different workbooks without causing any hindrances in the work.

Shared Workbooks

If you use Excel online, you can allow multiple users to edit the workbook at the same time. There is so much functionality that goes missing, which makes it a contender only for simple tasks. The shared workbook features in Excel will allow you to share the workbook between multiple users, but there are many restrictions. For instance, you cannot delete a group of cells or create a table in a shared workbook.

It is easy to walk around some restrictions, but for others, it is a matter of changing the structure of the entire workbook instead of using a workbook that has already been set up. These workarounds can, however, get in the way. As a result of this, it is impossible to use a workbook that is shared in the same way that you may use a single user workbook.

Any changes made in a shared workbook will be synchronized between the users every time the workbook is saved. These changes can be saved on a time schedule, meaning that a workbook can be saved or force saved every few minutes. The overhead of regular checking and savings every share user change is quite large. The size of the workbook can increase which will put a strain on your network, thereby slowing down every other system.

A shared workbook is prone to corruption. Microsoft office knows that this is the problem, but there is nothing much you can do about the issue. The alternative to this situation is to use Excel online since you can have multiple users working on the same workbook. Not many users will switch to excel online until Microsoft will remove all the restrictions on a shared workbook, and extend a multi-authoring tool to the Excel offline application.

Linked Workbooks

If you want to overcome the issue of multi-user editing, you should try to split the data across multiple workbooks. It is likely that these workbooks must be linked so that any value entered in one can be used in another. The links between workbooks also help to separate data using a logical method instead of using separate worksheets in one workbook.

Unfortunately, these links lead to instability and frustration. This is because the links need to be absolute or relative. In the case of absolute links, you will need to include the full path resource workbook while in the case of relative links, you only need to include the difference between the destination and source paths. This may sound sensible until you come across the rules the Excel decides to employ on when you can use each type of link, and when you can change them.

These rules are governed by numerous options. Some of these rules are dependent on whether the workbook was saved and whether it was saved before every link was inserted. There are times when Excel will automatically change the link when you open a workbook and use the save as option to copy the file. Excel may also change the links when you simply save the workbook down. One of the main disadvantages of using this option is that the links can break easily, and it is difficult to recover all the broken links. This is also a time-consuming affair since you cannot use the files that are affected by the broken links.

The linked data will only be updated when all the underlying files are open unless you edit links and update values. It is because of this that you may need to open 3 or 4 workbooks to ensure that all the information is flowing through in the right order. If you made a change in the value in the first workbook but open only the 3rd workbook, you will not see any changes because the second workbook still does not have the updated values.

It is logical to create a change in data, but this will increase the likelihood that the data is incorrect or/and when you open a workbook somebody else is already editing the underlying work. You can avoid the use of link workbooks, but there is a chance that you will end up entering the same data in more than one workbook. The danger with this is that you may type the data differently each time.

Data Validation

You must remember that any user can enter data on any computer system. People can transpose digits in numbers or mistype words with monotonous regularity. You must ensure that you check the data when it is entered or you will have a problem in the end.

Excel will always accept whatever any user types. Therefore, it is possible to set up a validation using lists, but it is impossible to maintain this list especially if that field is used in multiple places. For example, if a user should enter a customer reference number or a document ID they can enter the wrong record. To avoid this, it is always good to have some checks across the workbook. If there is no Data integrity, the system will be fatally compromised, which will affect the analysis.

You may already be suffering from this problem without having realized what the root cause is. Let us consider a situation where there is a list of invoices that you have entered in Excel Find the user has typed the name of every customer differently on every invoice. You got invoices to John limited, John Ltd and John. You are aware that these invoices point to the same company or customer, but Excel is not aware of this. This means that any analysis that you made using this data will always give you multiple results when they should only be one.

Navigation Issues

It is difficult to navigate through large workbooks. The number of sheet tabs in the bottom of the window is difficult to use and is a terrible way to find your way around the workbook. If there are many sheets in the workbook, and you cannot see all of them on the screen, it will be difficult for you to find what you are looking for. You can always click on the arrow to the left of your active sheet, but you will only see the first twenty sheets in that window. You cannot sort or group the list of sheets in any order.

Security Issues

You can add a lot of security features to an Excel workbook, but it is still going to have many problems. It is more important to work toward protecting the structure of the workbook, instead of worrying about the data. You can always lock some sheets and cells in the workbook to prevent some users from making any changes to the data or formulae. Regardless of whether you protect the sheet or not, if someone can see the data, they can make changes to it. You can avoid this by using some clever macro skills.

Speed Issues

You must remember that Excel is not the fastest application there is, and the programming language we use in Excel, VBA is slow and slightly sluggish when compared to the more professional languages like C and C#. This is because of the intended use of Excel and its flexibility. You should remember that Excel is a spreadsheet engine alone, and it can only be used to manage large volumes of data. This does not mean that you must always use Excel for this type of work. There are many other applications that you can use to perform such tasks since those applications were designed to perform these functions.

Enter the Database

If you are facing any of the issues that have been listed above, you should not ignore them. The answer or solution to these problems is to store the data in a structured manner. This means that we will need to start saving data in a database. This will allow you to think about your data in a logical manner. You have the ability to see how the data welding together and how you will need to interact with it to analyze the information.

You must, however, take heed. If you move from spreadsheets to databases, you should not duplicate the design of a spreadsheet. Instead, you should find a way to make the design better. There are some general database applications, listed below with which you can construct a simple solution. Alternatively, you can also use specialist database applications that allow you to switch from spreadsheet to databases within a few minutes point these applications are a better fit to big data.

For example, if you have a list of customers, their details, and any interaction you have had with these customers, then you should consider using a customer relationship management system. Customer relationship management system is a specialized database. Similarly, you can save accounts on packages like Sage and QuickBooks. There may be times when you cannot find an existing application to suit your needs. At such times you may need to build a database by yourself or request see IT department or any consultant to build the database for you.

The relational database is the most common type of database used in today's world. This database stores information or data in the form of tables which consists of columns and rows of data. Every row data will hold a separate item and every column will describe a different attribute of that item. For example, if the rows hold customer information, the columns can describe attributes like customer name and customer ID. All you need to do is enter the data once, and then you can use the same data to print on every invoice.

Every table in a relational database has a relationship between them. You can take the relationship between an invoice and the customer ID. Here you can always find an invoice that is related to a specific customer using the customer ID. Alternatively, you can also retrieve customer information from the invoice if necessary. All you need to do is enter the customer data of one in the database to create a record, and you can use that information across different invoices without having to type the data again. To use or create a database, you must define the tables and the relationships between those tables, and then define the type of layout you want to use to edit or list the data.

There are over a dozen applications that you can choose from. Some of the applications are easy to use and do the job for you. These applications will allow you to define the table, the data screen, and the reports. There are other applications that are more useful in specific areas but will require other tools to perform the job.

For example, some applications may be very powerful when comes defining a table and the relationship that table shares with the database and other tables, and it may also have some excellent analysis and reporting features. This application can, however, lack a tool which will allow you to define the data entry screen. An obvious example of such an application is Microsoft SQL. As is the case with large database systems, the SQL server will only take care of the back-end annual expect you to use, and other tools like visual studio to develop or maintain the front-end.

Choosing The Right Database

Access

Microsoft Access is one of the oldest databases available. This is easy to use and is extremely easy to abuse. You can design screens, reports, and tables from scratch or use an existing template. Some of the templates in Access do not teach you some good practices, but they will help you get started quickly. The programming and screen features and options are sophisticated, and you can deploy the application on the intranet without having to rely on sharing the files with users.

SharePoint

SharePoint is a document storage application and a database. This application can be used to compile and link simple lists. You can use the form designer to customize your dashboard, but it is important to remember that it is not a sophisticated application to use. SharePoint has the ability to suck the information from Excel and put it into a custom list. This makes it a useful application since everybody in your network will have access to the list. You can choose to add some security features which will restrict the access for some people. SharePoint can also send you an alert email when someone makes a change – adds, deletes or edits – to a record. You can also synchronize the information with Outlook if you have some data that concerns a person, calendar or task.

Zoho Creator

There is a database application that you can use in the Zoho office services available on the Internet. You can drag and drop the required layout in an easy way. This will also help you decide how the work should flow and what the interaction can be like. Since this is a web application, the data you use and the applications you develop can be found anywhere. Therefore, you should use the simple security features that this application provides to keep your data private. Zoho charges you per month but will allow you to store only some records depending on the price you choose to pay. If you want to use advanced features like email integration, you will need to pay an additional amount of money.

CHAPTER 14

How To Use Data From Excel

There are times when you will need to manually copy the data from one Excel file to the next. You can always automate this process if necessary, and also ensure that the data is copied correctly. You can also verify if the copied data has no duplications and no figure is entered into an incorrect location. This will help you save a lot of time.

You can either write the code in the Workbook_Open() event or include a function in the ThisWorkBook object to perform this function. When you write the code in the former event, the compiler will ensure that all the figures are copied over correctly when the source file is open.

When you want to develop the code, you should open the destination Excel file, and press the shortcut Alt+F8. The ThisWorkBook module can be found under the Microsoft Excel Objects in the Project Explorer window. You should now open the window and choose the "Workbook" object from the object dropdown[46].

---

[46] How to Get Values From Another Sheet in Excel Using VBA. (2019). Retrieved from https://chartio.com/resources/tutorials/how-to-get-values-from-another-sheet-in-excel-using-vba/

```
Option Explicit

Private Sub Workbook_Open()

   Call ReadDataFromCloseFile

End Sub

Sub ReadDataFromCloseFile()

         On Error GoTo ErrHandler

         Application.ScreenUpdating = False

         Dim src As Workbook

         ' OPEN THE SOURCE EXCEL WORKBOOK IN "READ
         ONLY MODE".

         Set src = Workbooks.Open("C:\Q-SALES.xlsx", True, True)

         ' GET THE TOTAL ROWS FROM THE SOURCE
         WORKBOOK.

         Dim iTotalRows As Integer

         iTotalRows = src.Worksheets("sheet1").Range("B1:B" &
         Cells(Rows.Count, "B").End(xlUp).Row).Rows.Count

         ' COPY DATA FROM SOURCE (CLOSE WORKGROUP)
         TO THE DESTINATION WORKBOOK.

         Dim iCnt As Integer     ' COUNTER.

         For iCnt = 1 To iTotalRows

      Worksheets("Sheet1").Range("B" & iCnt).Formula =

         src.Worksheets("Sheet1").Range("B" & iCnt).Formula
```

```
    Next iCnt

    ' CLOSE THE SOURCE FILE.

    src.Close False          ' FALSE - DON'T SAVE THE
    SOURCE FILE.

    Set src = Nothing

    ErrHandler:

    Application.EnableEvents = True

    Application.ScreenUpdating = True

End Sub
```

Property Application.ScreenUpdating

In the first line of the code, you will see that the Application.ScreenUpdating property is set to false. This will help you improve the speed of the macro that was written.

Open the Source File and Read Data

The next step is to open the source workbook that you are copying the information from. Remember that Excel will open the source file in the read only state, which will ensure that no changes are made to the source file.

```
Set src = Workbooks.Open("C:\Q-SALES.xlsx", True, True)
```

Once you have obtained the necessary information, the compiler will count the number of rows that are present in the source Excel workbook. This loop will run, and the data will be copied accurately from the source to the destination.

```
' COPY DATA FROM SOURCE (CLOSE WORKGROUP) TO THE DESTINATION FILE.

For iCnt = 1 To iTotalRows

   Worksheets("Sheet1").Range("B" & iCnt).Formula =

      src.Worksheets("Sheet1").Range("B" & iCnt).Formula

Next iCnt
```

Once the data has been copied over, you can set the property Application.ScreenUpdating to true.

CHAPTER 15

How to Manipulate Data In Excel

Every macro will process the code that is written in to manipulate and manage large volumes of data. The last chapter showed you how you can use VBA to format specific cells and fields in Excel to meet your criteria.

The following is an example of a VBA script:

```
Sub ConfigureLogic()

Dim qstEntries

Dim dqstEntries

Dim qstCnt, dqstCnt

qstEntries = Range("QualifiedEntry").Count

qst = qstEntries -
WorksheetFunction.CountIf(Range("QualifiedEntry"), "")

ReDim QualifiedEntryText(qst)

'MsgBox (qst)

dqstEntries = Range("DisQualifiedEntry").Count

dqst = dqstEntries -
WorksheetFunction.CountIf(Range("DisQualifiedEntry"), "")
```

```
ReDim DisqualifiedEntryText(dqst)

'MsgBox (dqst)

For qstCnt = 1 To qst

QualifiedEntryText(qstCnt) =
ThisWorkbook.Worksheets("Qualifiers").Range("J" & 8 +
qstCnt).value

'MsgBox (QualifiedEntryText(qstCnt))

logging ("Configured Qualified Entry entry #" & qstCnt & " as {" &
QualifiedEntryText(qstCnt) & "}")

Next

For dqstCnt = 1 To dqst

DisqualifiedEntryText(dqstCnt) =
ThisWorkbook.Worksheets("Qualifiers").Range("M" & 8 +
dqstCnt).value

'MsgBox (DisqualifiedEntryText(dqstCnt))

logging ("Configured DisQualified Entry entry #" & qstCnt & " as
{" & DisqualifiedEntryText(dqstCnt) & "}")

Next

includeEntry =
ThisWorkbook.Worksheets("Qualifiers").Range("IncludeSibling").v
alue

'MsgBox (includeEntry)

logging ("Entrys included in search - " & includeEntry)

End Sub
```

How to Analyze and Manipulate Data In A Spreadsheet

If you want to analyze data using VBA, you should look at the different macro settings in Excel. You must ensure that all the settings are as per the requirement. You must also ensure that every macro setting is activated in Excel. Now, you should create a worksheet and call it 'Qualifiers.' This is the worksheet that we will be using to ensure that the data is accurate and meets all the requirements. You can then set up the necessary qualifiers using the code that you have written. Remember that you cannot copy and paste these qualifiers, but will need to enter them into the system manually.

```
ThisWorkbook.Worksheets("Qualifiers").Range("J" & 8 +
qstCnt).value
```

How To Construct An Array And Locate The Range

In the above function, the range will start from Cell J9. The function notes 8, but the range is 9 since we have declared the qstCnt to be 1 using the following code:

```
For qstCnt = 1 To qst
```

It is because of this statement that the list will start at 9.

If you want to construct an array using the entries in the Qualifiers worksheet, you should add random words or numbers between cells J9 and J13, including those cells. When the rows are complete, you can find and manipulate the data in Excel.

```
Private Sub CountSheets()

Dim sheetcount

Dim WS As Worksheet

sheetcount = 0

logging ("*****Starting Scrub*********")
```

```
For Each WS In ThisWorkbook.Worksheets

sheetcount = sheetcount + 1

If WS.Name = "Selected" Then

'need to log the date and time into sheet named "Logging"

ActionCnt = ActionCnt + 1

logging ("Calling sheet: " & WS.Name)

scrubsheet (sheetcount)

Else

ActionCnt = ActionCnt + 1

logging ("Skipped over sheet: " & WS.Name)

End If

Next WS

'MsgBox ("ending")

ActionCnt = ActionCnt + 1

logging ("****Scrub DONE!")

Application.ScreenUpdating = True

End Sub
```

The following example will show you how you can write a macro for a working tab counter.

```
Dim sheetcount

Dim WS As Worksheet

sheetcount = 0
```

```
logging ("*****Starting Scrub*********")

For Each WS In ThisWorkbook.Worksheets

sheetcount = sheetcount + 1
```

When you initialize the sheet count variable, you should first set it to zero before you restart the counter. You can also use the logging() subroutine to keep track of all the actions in the qualifiers tab to make the correct selections. The For loop in the above example will set up the counting variable in the Active Workbook. Once you initialize WS, it will make the worksheet that you are currently in the active worksheet. Since this module is unnamed, it will run in any workbook. If you have many workbooks open, this module may run in an incorrect workbook. If you want to avoid any errors, you should name the workbook that you want the module to run in.

When the loop runs, it will add another variable to the sheet count and keep a track of the tabs. We will then move to

```
If WS.Name = "Selected" Then

'need to log the date and time into sheet named "Logging"

ActionCnt = ActionCnt + 1

logging ("Calling sheet: " & WS.Name)

scrubsheet (sheetcount)

Else

ActionCnt = ActionCnt + 1

logging ("Skipped over sheet: " & WS.Name)

End If
```

In this section of the code, we are trying to look for the Selected tab. VBA will run the subroutine if the variable WS is the same as the

Selected Worksheet. If the variable is not the same, the sheet will not be looked at by the compiler and the action will be looked at and counted. The code above is an example of how you can write macro to locate a specific tab or count the number of tabs in the macro.

In the next parts of this chapter, we will look at the different ways in which you can manipulate the data in Excel.

Different Ways To Manipulate Data

Count The Number Of Sheets In A Workbook[47]

Dim TAB

For Each TAB In ThisWorkbook.Worksheets

'some routine here

Next

Filter By Using Advanced Criteria

Range("A2:Z99").Sort key1:=Range("A5"), order1:=xlAscending, Header:=xlNo

Find The Last Column, Cell Or Row On A Worksheet

Dim cellcount

cellcount = Cells(ThisWorkbook.Worksheets("worksheet").Rows.Count, 1).End(xlUp).Row

Getting Values From Another Worksheet

---

[47] How To Manipulate Data in Excel Using VBA. (2019). Retrieved from https://ccm.net/faq/53497-how-to-manipulate-data-in-excel-using-vba

dim newvalue

newvalue = ThisWorkbook.Worksheets("worksheet").Range("F1").value

Apply Auto-Fit To A Column

Columns("A:A").EntireColumn.AutoFit

Adding Named Ranges to Specific Sheets

ThisWorkbook.Worksheets("worksheet").Names.Add Name:="Status", RefersToR1C1:="=worksheet!C2"

Insert Rows Into A Worksheet

Dim Row, Column

Cells(Row, Column).EntireRow.Select

Selection.Insert

Copy An Entire Row For Pasting

ActiveSheet.Range("A1").EntireRow.Select

Selection.Copy

Delete An Entire Row

ActiveSheet.Range("A1").EntireRow.Select

Selection.Delete

Inserting A Column Into A Worksheet

Dim Row, Column

Cells(Row, Column).EntireColumn.Select

Selection.Insert

Insert Multiple Columns Into A Worksheet

```
Dim insertCnt

Dim Row, Column

For insertCnt = 1 To N

ThisWorkbook.Worksheets("worksheet").Select

Cells(Row, Column).EntireColumn.Select

Selection.Insert

Next
```

Select A Specific Sheet

```
ThisWorkbook.Worksheets("worksheet").Select
```

Compare Values In A Range

```
Dim firstrange

Dim Logictest

Logictest = "some word or value"

If (Range(firstrange).value = Logictest) then

'some routine here

End If
```

CHAPTER 16

Resources For VBA Help

You cannot expect to become a VBA expert in a day. It is a journey and you will need to practice a lot before you become an expert. The best part about coding in Excel VBA is that there are many resources that you can use to improve your knowledge in Excel. This chapter covers some of the best places you can visit and some of the best resources you can use if you need a push in the right direction.

Allow Excel To Write The Code For You

If you have read the previous chapters, you know that you can use the macro recorder to help you with understanding your code. When you record any macro or the steps you want to automate using a record macro, Excel will write the underlying code for you. Once you record the code, you can review it and see what the recorder has done. You can then convert the code that the recorder has written into something that will suit your needs.

For instance, if you need to write a macro to refresh a pivot table or all pivot tables in your workbook and clear all the filters in the pivot table, it will get difficult to write the code from scratch. You can instead start recording the macro, and refresh every pivot table and remove all the filters yourself. When you stop recording the macro, you can review it and make the necessary changes to the code.

For a new Excel user, it would seem that the Help system is an add-in that always returns a list of topics that do not have anything to do with the topic you are looking for. The truth is that when you learn how to use the Help System correctly, it is the easiest and the fastest way to obtain more information about a topic. There are two basic tenets that you must keep in mind:

The Location Matters When You Ask For Help

There are two Help Systems in Excel: one that provides help on the different features in Excel and the other that provides information on some VBA programming topics. Excel will not perform a global search but will throw the criteria against the Help system which is in your current location. This means that you will receive the help that you need depending on which area of Excel you are working in. If you want help on VBA and macros, you need to be in the Visual Basic Environment (VBE) when you look for information. This will ensure that the keyword search is performed on the correct help system.

Choose Online Help Over Offline Help

When you look for some information on a topic, Excel will see if you are connected to the Internet. If your system is connected to the Internet, Excel will return results using some online content on Microsoft's website. Otherwise, Excel will use the help files that are stored offline in Microsoft office. It is always good to choose online help since the content is more detailed. It also includes updated information and the links to other resources that you can use.

Using Code From The Internet

The secret to building large programs is that you never have to write new code again. The macro syntax or the entire program that you want to use is certainly available on the Internet. This means that you never have to build anything from scratch. You can always use the code that is available on the Internet and apply that code to build different applications.

If you are stuck with creating or writing a macro for a specific task, all you need to do is describe the task you want to accomplish using Google Search. All you need to do is add the words "Excel VBA" before you describe your requirement.

For instance, if you want to write a macro that will allow you to delete all the blank rows in a worksheet, you should look for "How to delete blank rows in Excel using VBA?". You can bet a whole years' worth of salary that someone somewhere has already developed code for the same problem. There is probably an example that is available on the Internet which will give you an idea of what you need to do. This way you can simply build your own macro.

Leveraging Excel VBA User Forums

When you find yourself in trouble, you should post a question on a forum and then get guidance based on your requirement. A user forum is an online community that revolves around specific topics. You can ask numerous questions in these forums and get advice from experts on how you should solve some problems. The people answering your questions are volunteers who are passionate about helping the community solve some real-world problems.

There are many forums that are dedicated to helping people with Excel. If you want to find such a forum, you should type "Excel Forum" in Google Search. Let us look at some tips you can use to get the most out of the user form.

You should always read the forum and follow all the rules before you begin. These rules will often include some advice on how you should post your questions and also the etiquette you should follow.

Always check if the question you want to ask has already been answered. You should try to save some time by looking at the archives. Now, take a moment to look at the forum and verify if any of the questions you want answers to have already been asked.

You should use accurate and concise titles for any of your questions. You should never create a forum question using an abstract title like "Please Help" or "Need advice."

You should always ensure that the scope of your question is narrow. You should never ask questions like "How should I build an accounting macro in Excel."

You should always be patient, and remember that the people who are answering your questions are those who have a day job. You should always give the community sufficient time to answer the questions.

You should always check often when you post your questions. You will probably receive some information for more details about your question. You should always return to your post to either respond to some follow-up questions or review the answer.

You should always thank the person who has answered your question. If you were to receive an answer which helps you, you should thank the expert who has helped you.

Leveraging on Excel VBA Blogs And Articles

There are some dedicated Excel Gurus who have shared their knowledge through their blogs. These blogs are treasure troves of tricks and tips. They have some information that you can use to build your skills. The best part of using these blogs is that they are free to use.

These blogs do not necessarily answer your specific questions, but they offer many articles that you can use to advance your knowledge of VBA and Excel. These blogs can also provide some general guidance on how you can apply Excel in different situations. Let us look at a few popular Excel blogs:

ExcelGuru

ExcelGuru is a blog that was set up by Ken Puls. He is an Excel MVP who shares all his knowledge on his blog. Apart from the blog, Ken also offers many learning resources you can use to improve your knowledge in Excel.

Org

Org is a blog that was set up by Purna Chandoo Duggirala. He is an Excel expert from India who joined the scene in 2007. His blog offers innovative solutions and some free templates that will make you "awesome in Excel."

Contextures

Debra Dalgleish is the owner of a popular Excel website and is great with Microsoft Excel. She has included close to 350 topics on her website, and there will definitely be something that you can read.

DailyDose

The DailyDose is a blog that is owned by Dick Kusleika. It is the longest running Excel blog, and Dick is an expert at Excel VBA. He has written articles and blogs for over ten years.

MrExcel

Bill Jelen always uses Excel to solve any problems he has at work. He offers a large library of training resources and over thousands of free videos.

Mining YouTube For Some Excel VBA Training Videos

If you know that there are some training videos that are available on the Internet, and these sessions are better than articles, you should look for those videos. There are many channels that are run by amazing experts that are passionate for sharing knowledge. You will be pleasantly surprised to see the quality of those videos.

Attending A Live Online Excel VBA Training Class

Live training sessions are a great way to absorb good Excel knowledge form a diverse set of people. The instructor is providing some information on different techniques, but the discussions held after the class will leave you with a wealth of ideas and tips. You may have never thought of these ideas ever before. If you can survive these classes, you should always consider attending more of these sessions. Here are some websites that you can use for such sessions:

- Org
- ExcelHero
- ExcelJet
- Learning From The Microsoft Office Developer Center For Help With VBA

You should use the Microsoft Office Dev Center to get some help on how to start programming in Office products. The website is slightly difficult to navigate, but it is worth it to look at the sample code, free resources, step-by-step instructions, tools, and much more.

Dissecting Other Excel Files In Your Organization

Previous employees or current employees may have created files that already answer some of your questions. You should try to open different Excel files that contain the right macros, and also look at how these macros function. Then see how other employees in the organization develop macros for different applications. You should try not to go through the macro line-by-line but should look for some new techniques that may have been used.

You can also try to identify new tricks that you may have never thought of. You will probably also stumble upon some large chunks of code that you can implement or copy into your workbooks.

Ask The Local Excel Guru

Is there an excel genius in your department, company, community, or organization? If yes, you should become friends with that person now. That person will become your own personal guru. Excel experts love to share their knowledge, so you should never be afraid to approach an expert if you have any questions or want to seek advice on how you can solve some problems.

CHAPTER 17

Mistakes To Avoid

If you are reading this chapter, you will be familiar with Excel VBA. It is easy for anybody to make mistakes when they write a code in VBA. These mistakes will cost you greatly. This chapter lists the common mistakes that most VBA amateurs make.

Not Using Arrays

An interesting mistake that most VBA programmers make is that they try to process all the functions in a large nested loop. They filter the data down through the different rows and columns in the worksheet during the process of calculation. This method can work, but it can lead to performance troubles. If you have to perform the same function repeatedly, the efficiency of the macro will decrease. When you loop through the same column and you extract the values every single time, you are not only affecting the macro, but also affecting the processor. An efficient way to handle a list of numbers is to use an array.

If you have not used an array before, let me introduce it to you now. An array is a set of elements that have the same data type. Each element in the array is given an index. You must use this index to refer to the element in the array. An array can be defined by using the following statement: Dim MyArray (12) as Integer. This will create an array with 12 indices and variables that you will need to fill. Let us look at how a loop with an array will look[48] like:

```
Sub Test1()

    Dim x As Integer

    intNumRows = Range("A2",
    Range("A2").End(xldown)).Rows.Count

    Range("A2").Select

    For x = 1 To intNumRows

    arrMyArray(x-1) = Range("A" & str(x)).value)

    ActiveCell.Offset(1, 0).Select

    Next

End Sub
```

In this example, the code is processing through every cell in the range before it performs the calculation function.

Using .Select or .Activate

You do not have to always use the .Select or .Activate functions when you write code in VBA. You may want to use these functions since the Macro Recorder generates them. These functions are unnecessary for the following reasons:

- These functions may lead to the repainting of the screen. If you use the following function Sheets("Sheet1").Activate, Excel

[48] 7 Common VBA Mistakes to Avoid - Spreadsheets Made Easy. (2019). Retrieved from https://www.spreadsheetsmadeeasy.com/7-common-vba-mistakes-to-avoid/

will redraw the screen so you can see Sheet1. This will lead to a slow macro.

- These functions will confuse users since you will be manipulating the workbook when the user is working on it. There are some users who will worry that they are being hacked.

You should use these functions only when you want to bring the user to a specific cell or worksheet. Otherwise, you should delete the line of code since it will be doing more harm than good.

Using Variant Type

Another mistake that most programmers make is to use one Type when they are actually using another. If you look at the following code, you will think that a, b, and c are of the Long type. Well, that is incorrect since the variables a and b are of the Variant type. This means that they can be any data type, and can change from one type to another.

It is dangerous to have a variant type since it will become difficult for you to identify the bugs in your code. You should always avoid Variant types in VBA. There are some functions that will need the use of a Variant type, but you should avoid them if you can.

Not Using Application.ScreenUpdating = False

When you make a change to a cell or a group of cells in your code, Excel will need to repaint the screen to show the user the changes.

This will make your macros slow. When you write a macro the next time, you should use the following lines of code[49]:

```
Public Sub MakeCodeFaster()

        Application.ScreenUpdating = False


        ' Block of code

        ' This setting should always be reset back

        Application.ScreenUpdating = True

End Sub
```

Referencing the Worksheet Name With a String

[50]People will refer to a worksheet using a String. Look at the following example:

```
Public Sub SheetReferenceExample()

        Dim ws As Worksheet

        Set ws = Sheets("Sheet1")

        Debug.Print ws.Name

End Sub
```

---

[49] 7 Common VBA Mistakes to Avoid - Spreadsheets Made Easy. (2019). Retrieved from https://www.spreadsheetsmadeeasy.com/7-common-vba-mistakes-to-avoid/

[50] 7 Common VBA Mistakes to Avoid - Spreadsheets Made Easy. (2019). Retrieved from https://www.spreadsheetsmadeeasy.com/7-common-vba-mistakes-to-avoid/

This does seem harmless does it not. In most cases, it is harmless. Imagine that you give another person this workbook, and that person decides to rename the sheet to "Report." When he tries to run the macro, the macro will look for "Sheet1," which no longer exists. Therefore, this macro will not work. You should choose to reference the sheet by using an object instead of using the "Sheets" collection. To be more resilient, let us use the following block of code:

```
Public Sub SheetReferenceExample()

    Dim ws As Worksheet

    Set ws = Sheet1 ' used to be Sheets("Sheet1")

    Debug.Print ws.Name

End Sub
```

If you want to rename Sheet1 to something more meaningful, you can go to the VBA Project properties window and make a change to the name of the module. Once you rename the module, you will also need to update the VBA code.

Not Qualifying the Range References

[51]This is a common mistake that most people make when they write their code, and it is a real pain to debug this error. This error comes up when you do not qualify the range reference in the VBA code. You may wonder what I mean when I say range reference.

When you say Range("A1"), which sheet do you think the code is referring to? It is referring to the Activesheet. This means that the

---

[51] 7 Common VBA Mistakes to Avoid - Spreadsheets Made Easy. (2019). Retrieved from https://www.spreadsheetsmadeeasy.com/7-common-vba-mistakes-to-avoid/

compiler will look at cell A1 in the worksheet that the user is referring to. This is harmless on most occasions, but there are times when you may add more features to your code. These features make it hard for the compiler to execute the code. When the user or even you run the code, and you click on another worksheet, the code will behave differently. Let us look at the following example:

```
Public Sub FullyQualifyReferences()

    Dim fillRange As Range

    Set fillRange = Range("A1:B5")

    Dim cell As Range

    For Each cell In fillRange

    Range(cell.Address) = cell.Address

    Application.Wait (Now + TimeValue("0:00:01"))

    DoEvents

    Next cell

End Sub
```

Run the code in VBA and see what happens. If you do not specify the worksheet when you use the Range() function, Excel will assume that you are looking at the active sheet. To avoid this, you should make a slight change to your code. All you need to do is change Range(cell.Address) = cell.Address to Data.Range(cell.Address) = cell.Address.

In the second statement, data refers to the sheet object. There are other ways to do this, but I wanted to use a simple example which did not need the addition of too much code.

Writing a Big Function

If you go back to some of the old functions you may have written, you will notice that they are very long. You will need to continue to scroll until you reach the end of the function.

You should remember that the function you write should fit your screen. You should be able to view the code without having to scroll. You must ensure that you keep the methods short by creating sub procedures or helper functions.

Using Nested For or If Statements

[52]You may have read earlier that you can include many levels of nesting when you write your code. Do you think that is a good idea? You will need to add comments and indent the code to ensure that another user can read your code. If you are unsure of what I mean by nesting, let us look at the following example:

```
Public Sub WayTooMuchNesting()

    Dim updateRange As Range

    Set updateRange = Sheet2.Range("B2:B50")

    Dim cell As Range

    For Each cell In updateRange

    If (cell.Value > 1) Then

    If (cell.Value < 100) Then
```

[52] 7 Common VBA Mistakes to Avoid - Spreadsheets Made Easy. (2019). Retrieved from https://www.spreadsheetsmadeeasy.com/7-common-vba-mistakes-to-avoid/

```
            If (cell.Offset(0, 1).Value = "2x Cost") Then
            cell.Value = cell.Value * 2
            Else
            ' do nothing
            End If
        End If
        End If
        Next cell
End Sub
```

This is certainly not a clean code. If you use more than three levels of nesting, you have gone too far. To reduce the number of nesting levels, you should invert the condition in your If statement. In the example above, the code will make a change if a bunch of statements pass. You can invert this to ensure that the compiler will only execute the statements for the opposite case. That way you can skip the many levels of nesting.

Let us look at the updated[53] version of the above example.

```
Public Sub ReducedNesting()
        Dim updateRange As Range
   Set updateRange = Sheet2.Range("B2:B50")
```

---

[53] 7 Common VBA Mistakes to Avoid - Spreadsheets Made Easy. (2019). Retrieved from https://www.spreadsheetsmadeeasy.com/7-common-vba-mistakes-to-avoid/

```
Dim cell As Range
For Each cell In updateRange
If (cell.Value <= 1) Then GoTo NextCell
If (cell.Value >= 100) Then GoTo NextCell
If (cell.Offset(0, 1).Value <> "2x Cost") Then GoTo NextCell
cell.Value = cell.Value * 2
NextCell:
Next cell
End Sub
```

You can also combine the If statements in the code above if you wish.

Conclusion

On that note, we have come to the end of this book. I want to thank you once again for purchasing the book and I sincerely hope you find it informative.

This book will help you gain a good understanding of what VBA is and how you can use it to automate processes in Excel. The book also helps you understand how you can fix code or handle errors.

I hope this book helps you automate the many processes that you do in Excel.

Good Luck!

References

(2019). Retrieved from http://users.iems.northwestern.edu/~nelsonb/IEMS435/VBA Primer.pdf

10 Resources for Excel VBA Help - dummies. (2019). Retrieved from https://www.dummies.com/software/microsoft-office/excel/10-resources-for-excel-vba-help/

7 Common VBA Mistakes to Avoid - Spreadsheets Made Easy. (2019). Retrieved from https://www.spreadsheetsmadeeasy.com/7-common-vba-mistakes-to-avoid/

9 quick tips to improve your VBA macro performance. (2019). Retrieved from https://techcommunity.microsoft.com/t5/Excel/9-quick-tips-to-improve-your-VBA-macro-performance/td-p/173687

Banik, A. (2019). Excel VBA – Read Data from a Closed Excel File or Workbook without Opening it. Retrieved from https://www.encodedna.com/excel/copy-data-from-closed-excel-workbook-without-opening.htm

Conditional Logic in VBA. (2019). Retrieved from http://codevba.com/learn/condition_statements.htm#.W-UNZ5MzbIU

Conditional Statements in Excel VBA - If, Case, For, Do Loops. (2019). Retrieved from https://analysistabs.com/excel-vba/conditional-statements/

Conditional Statements in Excel VBA - If, Case, For, Do Loops. (2019). Retrieved from https://analysistabs.com/excel-vba/conditional-statements/

Error Handling In VBA. (2019). Retrieved from http://www.cpearson.com/excel/errorhandling.htm

Excel Macro Troubleshooting Tips. (2019). Retrieved from https://www.contextures.com/excelvbatips.html

Excel VBA - Introduction. (2019). Retrieved from https://www.tutorialspoint.com/excel_vba_online_training/excel_vba_introduction.asp

Excel VBA Loops, with examples. For Loop; Do While Loop; Do Until Loop. (2019). Retrieved from http://www.globaliconnect.com/excel/index.php?option=com_content&view=article&id=122:excel-vba-loops-with-examples-for-loop-do-while-loop-do-until-loop&catid=79&Itemid=475

Excel VBA Primer. (2019). Retrieved from http://ce270.groups.et.byu.net/syllabus/vbaprimer/intro/index.php

Excel VBA Tutorial Introduction: How to get started. (2019). Retrieved from http://www.easyexcelvba.com/introduction.html

Getting Started With VBA — The Spreadsheet Guru. (2019). Retrieved from https://www.thespreadsheetguru.com/getting-started-with-vba/

Gomez, J. (2019). Excel VBA Sub Procedures: The Complete Tutorial. Retrieved from https://powerspreadsheets.com/vba-sub-procedures/

Gomez, J. (2019). VBA Loops Explained: Complete Tutorial On 6 Essential Excel VBA Loops. Retrieved from https://powerspreadsheets.com/excel-vba-loops/#What-Is-An-Excel-VBA-Loop

Kelly, P. (2019). How to Easily Extract From Any String Without Using VBA InStr - Excel Macro Mastery. Retrieved from https://excelmacromastery.com/vba-instr/#Example_3_Checkif_a_filename_is_valid

Kelly, P. (2019). The Ultimate Guide to VBA String Functions - Excel Macro Mastery. Retrieved from https://excelmacromastery.com/vba-string-functions/#How_To_Use_Compare

Kelly, P. (2019). The Ultimate Guide to VBA String Functions - Excel Macro Mastery. Retrieved from https://excelmacromastery.com/vba-string-functions/#Searching_Within_a_String

Loop in Excel VBA. (2019). Retrieved from https://www.excel-easy.com/vba/loop.html

Mathier, S. (2019). VBA Course: Introduction. Retrieved from https://www.excel-pratique.com/en/vba/introduction.php

MS Excel: How to use the IF-THEN-ELSE Statement (VBA). (2019). Retrieved from https://www.techonthenet.com/excel/formulas/if_then.php

Read or Get Data from Worksheet Cell to VBA in Excel - ANALYSISTABS - Innovating Awesome Tools for Data Analysis!. (2019). Retrieved from https://analysistabs.com/excel-vba/read-get-data-from-cell-worksheet/

String Manipulation in Excel VBA. (2019). Retrieved from https://www.excel-easy.com/vba/string-manipulation.html

Strings in VBA. (2019). Retrieved from http://codevba.com/learn/strings.htm#.W-RAHNUzaCg

Ten VBA Tips and Tricks. (2019). Retrieved from http://what-when-how.com/excel-vba/ten-vba-tips-and-tricks/

Variables in Excel VBA. (2019). Retrieved from https://www.excel-easy.com/vba/variables.html

VBA Conditional Statements. (2019). Retrieved from https://www.excelfunctions.net/vba-conditional-statements.html

VBA Loops - For, Do-While and Do-Until Loops. (2019). Retrieved from https://www.excelfunctions.net/vba-loops.html

VBA Primer (Excel). (2019). Retrieved from http://mcise.uri.edu/jones/ise325/vba%20primer.htm

VBA Strings. (2019). Retrieved from https://www.tutorialspoint.com/vba/vba_strings.htm

VBA Sub Procedure. (2019). Retrieved from https://www.tutorialspoint.com/vba/vba_sub_procedure.htm

Wells, R. (2019). Declaring Variables in VBA - wellsr.com. Retrieved from https://wellsr.com/vba/excel/vba-declare-variable/

EXCEL MACROS

The Ultimate Beginner's Guide to Learn Excel Macros Step-by-Step

David A. Williams

Introduction

Planning, organizing, estimating, and calculating to create better financial data used to be a tedious job that individuals had to perform manually. Many responsibilities, including bookkeeping, payroll creation, computation, etc. require calculative formats that need to be strictly accurate for productivity. Without a proper tool to help with these official responsibilities, a professional could not have survived.

Along came tools like Microsoft Excel, which have saved a lot of crucial time for professionals. Excel has been used for quite a while, and it surely has advanced to a level where it has become a necessity for all types of businesses. That is why learning it is important.

However, there is another side of Excel besides the usual calculative tools and tabular layouts that it is capable of. That side is known as Excel Macros. With an intention to educate the regular Excel users, this book will help readers understand about Macros. The purpose of this book is to help people get familiar with the world of macros.

Many are interested in Macros while going through Excel, but they feel scared to learn it because of the formula-based syntax it possesses, which feels like coding. If you want to learn Excel coding or have decided to try some projects that need the help of Macros, then this book is here to guide you.

Assuming that you do not have any knowledge about Microsoft Excel at all, we would like to first start with a couple of basic chapters to learn about this spreadsheet program in brief. Once that is complete, we will move on to the part where you will learn about basic Macros strategies, etc.

Note that, this book will cover Macros in later chapters with a vision to make you knowledgeable of its fundamentals in detail. It will also elaborate on the various uses, benefits, tips, and other basic aspects related to this coding side of Excel. However, you may have to go through other sources at later stages if you are willing to learn about its advance applications. For now, continue reading through the chapters one by one and learn about Microsoft Excel, Macros, and its fundamentals.

CHAPTER 1

Learning About Microsoft Excel

As mentioned earlier, MS Excel is a program designed for spreadsheets. This program is one of the most useful applications designed by Microsoft for its Windows operating system.

Since the day it has existed, it has been revamped and updated to provide you with tons of features, including macro coding, calculation, graphing tools, tables, pivot tables, etc. You get this tool as a sub-application of the bundle tool under the name Microsoft Office. You may already be aware of other MS Office applications like MS Word and MS PowerPoint. But, MS Excel is not the only spreadsheet program that developers created. Other programs that have spreadsheet features include Lotus 1, 2, and 3.

In MS Excel, you can see the layout designed with a grid comprising of cells, where you can use your keyboard to input data, such as texts, numbers, symbols, and other characters. The most common uses that Excel has are in scheduling, budgeting for home or office, accounting, and similar areas. Without it to help a professional, he or she would have taken loads of time to compute the data.

For people dealing with statistics, engineering, and finance, this application is a boon, as it helps them create histograms, charts, and reports, easily. Thus, its high usability has made it gain popularity as one of the most preferable applications on the globe. In some cases, people have been known to use Excel over MS PowerPoint or MS Word for their daily data creation, computation, and other features just because it is more versatile than the latter.

Basic Excel Operations

Now, this section will help you understand some of the basic operations that you can use in Excel. Maybe you are knowledgeable of them beforehand after using Excel beforehand. But, keeping in mind the various skills levels of the readers, this section will help you all refresh the features once again.

Furthermore, you will also learn about some shortcuts that you can use for basic operations in Excel in this section. Always remember that learning and applying shortcuts will improve your efficiency to complete your work on Excel sheets faster.

- **Creating A New Excel Workbook**

  To start using Excel, you need to first start by creating a workbook. A workbook in Excel usually has three sheets. For creating a new workbook, you can move to the File tab in the upper-left corner of your computer and click on the New button from the ribbon (ribbon will be discussed in later chapters). Alternatively, you can simply press the shortcut key combination: Ctrl + N to get started with a new workbook.

- **Opening An Existing Workbook**

  In some cases, you may want to view an existing workbook in Excel. For that, you can press the Open button from File tab. This will pop up a dialog box in which you can look for the file you want to open. You should be aware of the extensions Excel uses, which are: .XLS (for older Excel) and .XLSX (for newer Excel versions). Alternatively, you have the shortcut key combination to open the dialog window using Ctrl + O keys.

A third technique is also there to open an Excel workbook. In this method, you can first open Excel normally, and then search for the file you want to open in your drive. Just drag and drop that file onto the opened Excel application. Excel will then open the file for you.

- **Saving A Workbook or File in Excel**

After you have added your data in the sheets of your workbook, you can use the Save option from the File tab in your application. When you are saving the file for the very first time, Excel will notify you with a dialog box where you can enter the name of your workbook. You also get to choose the location for your file. The shortcut key for saving the file is Ctrl + S. This will let you save the file.

Furthermore, if you have already saved the file once and named it, then pressing the save button or Control + S keys will just write the updated data on your existing saved file. This will not offer any kind of dialog box to rename the file. There is another shortcut key that you can use for saving your file instantly, which is F12.

To notify you that the file is being saved, you will see a loading bar flash on the bottom bar of the Excel application. Another way by which your computer notifies you of a save in progress is through an hourglass symbol.

- **Printing Spreadsheets in Excel**

Often you require printing the created spreadsheets in Excel just like other Office applications. You can do that by using the Print option from the File tab menu. This will open up a window with the printing options for your sheet.

The other way is through a shortcut key which is Control + P. The dialog box that opens can be used for selecting the number of copies you want to print for your workbook. The box will also let you choose the page range in your created sheet, which you want your printer to process.

Note that the newer Excel versions do not pop up with a dialog box for the print button. Pressing the Print button takes you to another menu categorized under the File tab menu.

Plus, if you want to view how the print will appear before printing it, you can do that by pressing the key combination: Ctrl + F2. Pressing this combination in a newer version of Excel will take you to the sub-menu for Print option, which has the preview of the print for your file.

- **Page Layout Feature In Excel**

The newer versions of Excel also offer a feature where you can preview your page present inside the workspace region. This can be done using the Page Layout option. You can access this button through the View tab menu present on the top bar. Another alternative to view this Page Layout option is by clicking it from the right lower corner of your computer screen. You can find it right next to the slider for zooming your page.

- **Closing Workbooks and Excel**

After you have finished working on your workbook in Excel, you may feel like closing it with the complete application. Moreover, you may feel like closing the workbook that you have opened currently and switch it with a new one.

For closing a workbook that is open, you can visit the File tab menu, and press the Close button present in the options. The shortcut key that you can use for closing the file is Ctrl + W.

Closing will cause the Excel to enter a state where several of its functions become dormant, as there is no sheet to operate. Note that if you have not saved your sheets, and have pressed the Close button, then Excel will notify you with a dialog box that informs you whether you want to save the file or close it without saving. Here you get the chance to save the file and name it or just cancel it without saving.

Once the workbook is closed, you can simply add a new workbook, open an existing one, or close the complete application by clicking on the cross button in the upper right corner. The shortcut key for closing Excel is Alt + F4. You can also use the taskbar of your computer to close the application by right clicking on it and selecting the Exit option.

CHAPTER 2

Using the Ribbon And Other Common Functions

Now that you are familiar with the use of basic operations of Excel, it is time to move to the functions that are commonly used in Excel. Plus, this chapter will help you familiarize with Excel ribbon.

MS Excel has been classified into two categories:

1. The older versions that lack the ribbon
2. The newer versions that have the ribbon

So what is the Ribbon?

It is a layout that has been offered to the tool bar and the File tab menu bar. The older version of Excel and similar MS applications had a simple drop-drown menu with all the relevant functions. However, the newer versions have a list of options accessible through a dynamic layout, which modifies the toolbar content present below it or the body of the ribbon. This layout is quite simplistic and has been able to efficiently organize all the tools without taking too much space like the older versions.

Microsoft Office also lets you disable the ribbon look by pressing the Ctrl + F1 keys to hide it from the layout of your Excel application. Similarly, pressing the keys again will bring the ribbon back. If you do not want to use your mouse cursor to choose the various functions present in the ribbon, then you can use the Alt key combined with the highlighted alphabet in the ribbon as an alternative to navigating through the various tools (which can be done using the Tab key).

This can be done by pressing the Alt key, which will prompt Excel to offer you with tool tips next to each of the tool buttons and menu options. These tools tips have the various alphabets as mentioned earlier. Pressing the letter will take you to the section of the ribbon that you want to access.

For instance, if you want to use the Review section, then you can press the Alt key followed by the alphabet R, which is the alphabet assigned to the Review section. This will give you access to all the functions under the Review section display within the ribbon. After showing the Review section, the tool buttons will have the tooltips with them. As mentioned earlier, you can also navigate using the Tab key. Pressing it will highlight a button that is currently selected. Pressing Tab repeatedly will cycle through all the option in the ribbon for you to choose. You can press Enter at the highlighted option that you want to access.

- **Using Help In Excel**

  Times will come where you will feel confused about a function or an operation. Moreover, there will be situations where you may not recall the correct way of using a tool in Excel. When this happens, and you are not even online to take help from your search engine, then you may want to utilize Excel Help for aiding you. The Help option is accessible with the help F1 key on your keyboard.

Alternatively, you can use the Help option is by clicking it from the File tab menu. With the Help window, you will have access to all the basic operations and commands in Excel. You can also learn about advance features, steps and tips for troubleshooting, etc. All of these will make you more efficient and quicker while working in this application. Plus, using the Help window is easy as you can simply search for your query to highlight it in front of you on the screen.

- **Redo And Undo**

Just like in other MS Office applications, Excel too provides with the ability to redo and undo your input data. For using undo, you just need to press the key combination: Ctrl + Z. Furthermore, if you plan to redo your recent input, then you can just press the combination: Ctrl + Y.

Alternatively, the redo and undo functions can be performed directly by the Redo and Undo buttons present in the top left corner of Excel. Clicking either of these buttons will perform its relevant action. Moreover, these buttons will also let you see all the redo and undo actions you have performed in your workbook. This feature will offer you the ease of performing multiple redo and undo actions.

- **Copy, Cut, and Paste**

Another group of basic operations that are found on Excel, just like other MS Office applications, are the copy, cut, and paste functions. You can use the following shortcut keys to perform these functions:

Ctrl + C for Copy

Ctrl + X for Cut

Ctrl + V for Paste

Furthermore, you can access these from the context menu (accessible with the right click on your mouse). You can access it when you click on a specific cell on the sheet.

CHAPTER 3

Navigating Through Cells

Note that most of your time on Excel will be about editing and navigating cells. Using the help of just your mouse will not be a very time-efficient method of working on your project. To avoid consuming unnecessary time while working on this application, you will have to learn the shortcuts needed for navigating through cells.

Cell Navigation Fundamentals

With the help of the cursor keys, you can move around the Excel cells. As mentioned earlier, you can also use your mouse to click on cells, which you want to choose and edit. However, using a mouse will be a daunting task in cases where you have to deal with a large amount of data and multiple pages.

- **Navigating Quickly Through Sheets**

  As you keep inputting data on your sheet, you will have a considerable amount of data filled up on it. Unluckily, you will not be able to see all the cells on which you input or edit data, as the viewport has a limited view.

  Besides the use of the cursor keys to navigate around each cell on the sheet, you can also use the Page Down and Page Up buttons on your keyboard to view cells that are not visible in your viewport. These buttons, which are highlighted as PgDn and PgUp, can help you move down and up the screen at a much faster rate. This can be a much convenient way of working on the sheet if you get used to it.

Similarly, moving your cursor quickly towards the left can be done by pressing the Page Up button with the Alt button at the same time. And, for moving fast towards the right, you can press the Page Down button with the Alt button.

In specific situations, you can even use the End and Home buttons on your keyboard to move from the bottommost to the topmost cell of your sheet. Press the Alt button with either of the buttons will help you navigate to the extreme left or right cell in the currently highlighted row of your sheet.

You can also press the End button to bring the Excel into End mode, in which pressing the arrow key or cursor will take the user to the specific edge of the data region. This edge is highlighted with respect to the direction arrow key pressed.

- **Navigating Around The Edge of the Data Region**

In some situations, you will have to navigate your cursor to accurately reach the edge of a cluster of data. Note that this edge is not the end cell of the sheet, but the last cell containing the data input by you. For that, you can use the Ctrl combined with the cursor buttons.

For instance, think of a table of 4 x 4 that you have created with data filled in it. By pressing Ctrl + Down arrow key, you can move the cursor to the bottommost cell with data in it. Similarly, you can navigate around the created table by combining the Ctrl key and the any of the arrow keys.

As a reminder, the key combination explained above will work only on rows and columns that are fill with consistent data. If you find an empty cell between the input data, then the cursor will just navigate to the cell before the empty cell, and not cross over to the next cell with data.

- **Highlighting Multiple Cells**

For highlighting many cells at the same time in your worksheet, you can use the left mouse button with the Ctrl key. For this, you need to hold the Ctrl button and then keep clicking the cells that you want to highlight together.

A second method that can be used for this is by pressing the Shift key with the F8 button. When you press these buttons together, your application will enable the Multi-select mode. You will see it highlighted in the status bar and know that the mode is now enabled for you to apply it.

You can see the words Add to Selection highlighted there when the correct key combinations are pressed. If you want to end this mode, then you can do it by pressing the Esc button on your keyboard.

- **Extension of Selected Cells**

For selecting multiple cells in a column or row, you can use the Shift key combined with the relevant cursor button to move around and add the cells adjacent to it.

- **Selecting Cells Until The Edge Of The Data Area**

You can also select the complete column or row containing data by pressing the combination Ctrl + Shift + any of the directional keys to highlight all the cells until the edge of the data region.

- **Selecting Cells Extending To The Next Screen**

  As you may have already seen, you are following a pattern when you are using an extension of selected cells. On combining the Shift key with the directional key, you are able to highlight multiple cells at once. If you just want to select random cells at once, then you will have to hold the Ctrl button and click the specific cells.

  Extending the selection to the next screen can be performed by pressing the Shift key with the Page Up or Page Down button. For going left or right side, you can press the Alt button with the combination discussed in the previous sentence.

- **Navigating Around Active Cells**

  If you have been editing a cell currently or have a highlighted cell and you want to navigate the cursor to the cell next to it, then you can do it with the help for the Shift, Tab, and Enter keys. Here is how it will work:

  1. Pressing Shift + Tab keys will navigate the cursor to the left cell.
  2. Pressing Tab key will let you move the cursor to the right cell.
  3. Pressing Shift + Enter keys will let you navigate the cursor to the cell on top.
  4. Pressing Enter will let you move the cursor to the cell at the bottom.

Another way of doing this navigation activity is by just selecting the F8 button. This will cause Excel to enter the Extended Selection mode. Entering this mode will let you navigate to extend the selected cells using the direction keys.

CHAPTER 4

Formatting Functions and Shortcuts

By now, you are familiar with the fundamentals of Excel. You will notice that your speed and efficiency while using this application has improved considerably. Your efficiency may have been further improved if you are using the shortcut key combinations subconsciously. This way, you can shorten the time you take to work on the sheets.

Text Formatting Fundamentals in Excel

After you have been able to master the combinations and navigation tools from the previous chapters, your next basic tutorial is to learn about the fundamentals of formatting text in Excel. Here are a couple of easy and common shortcut combinations for formatting text in this application.

1. To start with the formatting of a specific text, you can highlight the text or click on the particular cell that you want to be formatted. For making the text bold in a particular cell, you can press Ctrl + B keys.

2. To italicize the text, you can press the combination: Ctrl + I.

3. To underline the text in the cell, you can highlight the cell and pressing the combination: Ctrl + U.

4. If you want to use a strikethrough, you can press the combination: Ctrl + 5.

You can also cancel any of the formatting tools on your text by repeating the combination key once again. If you want the same formatting to be done on another cell, then just highlight that particular cell, and press F4 key on that cell. It will cause the cell to be formatted to the same style as you did for the previous cell.

Dialog Box For Formatting

There is also a dialog box that lets you get access to all the common formatting options at one place and that too quickly. This can be accessed by pressing the Ctrl + 1 keys, which will let you edit the cell for appropriate styling.

This dialog box for formatting will let you format the text, align it, change the style of font, alter the border of the cell, etc. If you just need to modify the font of the text in the cell, then you can do that by pressing the combination: Ctrl + Shift + F. Note that, this combination will also let you access the dialog box for formatting, but it will also automatically select the font tab.

You can alternatively use the Ribbon, which comprises of more styling and formatting options than the dialog box. Accessing options other than the common ones is much convenient to access from the Ribbon.

Adding or Editing a Comment In a Cell

At times you will be working with a colleague on a sheet or workbook. In such cases, you may need to comment or add notes to a particular cell or cells so that the other person can be notified of your comment. This is a significant method for the people who are not present to work on the same document at the same physical place. With its help, you have the benefit of tracking all the changes made to the sheet efficiently. You also have the ability to use comments as indicators that is important when the workbook comprises of a huge amount of data filled in hundreds of columns and rows.

In addition, comments will also act as reminders for you if you want them to notify you at later stages while going through the sheet.

You can add a comment with the key combination: Shift + F2. Pressing this combination will highlight a small yellow-colored box, which will stay active at the corner of the cell. This box can be used to leave any notes or comments. Moreover, you can also look at existing notes or comments, which you can edit as well.

After adding a comment to a particular cell, you will notice a red-colored arrow appearing on the top right corner of the cell border. To see the comment or note on that cell, you will have to hover your mouse's cursor on that cell. Also, if you want to see all the cells that have been commented on, then you can press the key combination Ctrl + Shift + O. This will cause all the cells with a comment to highlight.

Adding Time and Date to Cells

Another option that you can try out on cells is adding time and date. This means that you can set the current time and date to a specific cell. This can be done using the Ctrl + ; keys.

Cloning the Value In Cells

For duplicating or cloning the cell values, you will have to first highlight the existing cell with the value, and then press the keys Ctrl + Shift + ‘.

Adding Hyperlinks to Cells

Adding hyperlinks to text or cells can be done by pressing the combination: Ctrl + K. Upon doing that, you will see a dialog box appear on the screen for the hyperlink. You can add the URL that you want the cell to link to.

Setting For Text Alignment And Other Shortcut Keys Using Alt Button

To modify the alignment of the text for a cell, you can use several key combinations. For instance, to align the cell text in the center of the cell, you need to first hold the Alt key. After that, you have to press H, A, & C. This is just a simple shortcut that you are using for the options present in the Ribbon.

Technically, holding Alt and then pressing H, will highlight the Home tab on the Ribbon. After that, pressing A will toggle the toolbar's alignment options. And, pressing the C key will trigger the align center function. You can press the Alt key to review the assigned alphabets to the various functions on the Ribbon.

Similarly, you can use similar formatting functions, which you can locate on the Home tab or other tabs in Excel's Ribbon.

Working with Tables

Tables have a significant use in various workbooks and sheets. However, most users are not using tables in Excel to that much extent. For creating a table in your workbook, you can simply press the combination: Ctrl + T.

To navigate to a row on your created table, you can press Shift + Spacebar. Alternatively, you can navigate to a column by pressing the Ctrl + Spacebar. For selecting your complete table, you can press Ctrl + A together.

CHAPTER 5

Introduction To Macros

Before starting with Macros, it is advisable that you first go through the other basic functions, layout, and options of Excel. Figuring out the Excel formulae will help you be aware of Macros and its uses in a much more efficient way. Plus, it will be easier for you to learn the advanced stages of Macros when you decide to move to the next level in Excel.

Nevertheless, there is no rule stating that you cannot learn Macros without going through the basic functions of Excel.

So, What are Macros?

If there are multiple tasks to be carried out in MS Excel, and that too in repetition, then you will need the help of macros. Macros are considered to be a cluster of actions that you can execute as many times as you want.

Sometimes you need to repeat certain tasks and functions in Excel. For a couple of rows or columns, this may still be manageable. But, if you have multiple sheets on which you have to apply a repeated number of functions, this can be tedious.

With the help of a macro, you are automating the process. As a result, you are saving your time. So, a macro can be defined as an action or actions, which you can execute several times as you feel like. Upon creating a macro, you are technically recording the keystroke and mouse clicks. Once you have created a macro, you can format it later as per your needs and requirements. Its extension is referred to as .MAC.

Macros comprise of a code that will initialize your work automatically in an application. It will let you add customized improvements and features to help you in fulfilling a task at a faster rate. And, all you will need to execute it is a click of a button. For applications involving spreadsheets, macros are a robust tool.

Think of a situation where you have to develop a monthly report for an accounting assignment. You will need to edit the names of all the consumers with accounts that are overdue in yellow color. Plus, you are tasked with adding bold styling to all the text. With the help of a macro, you can apply all these styling functions instantly.

The usual macro processor used for various purposes is a universal purpose macro process that is not integrated or connected with a particular software or language type. Macro processors are codes that let you copy a specific set of text commands from one place to another to replace it and automate the process.

Several ways exist in which macros are executed in MS Excel. Furthermore, macros are the official coding language assigned to Excel. This coding language is known as VBA, which is the short form of Visual Basic for Applications. Note that VBA is not the same as Visual Basic. The latter language is a core programming language that is required to create various programs, which users use for various applications. Visual Basic lets you create files with the extension .exe and you can execute these files in the Windows OS.

On the other hand, VBA is a different type of coding language. It does not have the ability to create independent programs or applications. You will have to use the help of an MS Office application (which is not just limited to MS Excel). In other words, VBA is a small part of Visual Basic, as both languages have a similar approach but the former only runs in MS Office applications.

In addition, a macro can be considered a tool that offers permission to add various functions in reports, controls, and forms besides performing tasks automatically. For example, the OnClick feature of a button is linked with a macro to initiate a particular set of commands every time a user presses that button.

On considering Access, you can assume macros to be a fundamental coding language that you code by creating a group of actions to run. On the development of a macro, you are selecting that particular action from a dropdown list that appears. After that, you enter all the relevant fields to perform each action.

Furthermore, macros give you the authority to process controls, forms, and reports without the need for advanced coding like in Visual Basic. VBA applications just focus on a subclass of commands that you can use for creating macros in Excel and similar applications. This way, it becomes much easier to learn and use macros for people who find it hard to understand and learn VBA codes.

You can easily access VBA in Excel. This coding language is a 4th generation coding language. Consider each generation to be an evolved language with the solution to confusing and unrecognizable symbols. It is quite easy to understand 4GL (4th gen languages).

For instance, check this code out:

Selection.Font.Bold = True

Even if you are not familiar with coding, you will still be able to figure out what this code is capable of doing. It will help you bold your selection. It may feel a little weird on first glance, but you will get used to this format.

For your reference and comparison with a core programming language, here is a C++ program. Have a look at it and see how tough it is compared to VBA.

```
printf("%d:%0d\n",tmp->tm_hour,tmp->min);
```

This C++ code will print the time in hours and minutes.

Surely, it will be hard for a layman to understand what all these characters and symbols mean. So, be thankful that you do not have to deal with coding in this language to work on Excel.

Building a UserForm for Excel

One of the things that you can do using Visual Basic Editor is create a UserForm. What exactly is a UserForm? It is a custom dialog box that you can create to help you with certain purposes.

When you use a UserForm, you can enable a convenient interface in your sheet or document, allowing you to enter data in a more controllable manner. This makes the data easier to view and use, both for you and other users of the sheet.

How to Build the Form

Open Excel and then start the Visual Basic Editor. You can use the keyboard shortcut of ALT + F11; this shortcut is set by default unless you have modified it, in which case, you have to use the modified version of the shortcut. You will also need to use both the Properties Window and the Project Explorer. You can easily find these features in the View drop-down menu.

One of the things that you should remember before working on a UserForm is that you should try not to double-click on anything, unless you have been given specific instructions to do so. The reason for this is that double-clicking opens a code window. If you do double-click, then worry not. You do not have to close the sheet to restart everything! All you have to do is close the code window by clicking on the Close button. You can alternatively choose to switch back to the UserForm design window by using the appropriate keyboard shortcut (by default, it is always ALT + TAB).

Head over to the Project Explorer and ensure that you have selected the current sheet that you are working on as the workbook. Then head over to the Insert Menu and then select UserForm.

Once you do this, you will notice that a new blank UserForm pops up within the Visual Basic Editor.

You should also be able to see a Toolbox. However, if such a box does not appear, then all you have to do is go to the View menu and select the Toolbox option.

You may notice that the UserForm has a dotted border surrounding it. This border can be expanded. By doing this, you will be able to change the dimensions of the UserForm.

Remember that a single sheet could contain multiple UserForms. This is why it is vital that you give appropriate names for each of the UserForms for the purpose of identification.

Now you can get down to adding textboxes and labels into your UserForm.

To add a textbox, choose the TextBox button in the Toolbox and then click on any area of the form that you would like to add your text. You will be given resizing handles. These handles provide you with the ability to resize the TextBox as your see fit.

Now, you can add multiple controls into the TextBox. For the purpose of this example, let us go right ahead and use the below controls within the TextBox:

TextBox - Name: txtLastName

Label - Caption: Last Name:

CommandButton - Name: cmdOK, Caption: OK

TextBox - Name: txtDate

Label - Caption: Date:

Label - Caption: Amount:

CommandButton - Name: cmdClear, Caption: Clear

ComboBox - Name: cboDepartment

Label - Caption: Department:

TextBox - Name: txtAmount

CheckBox - Name: chkReceipt, Caption: Receipt?

CommandButton - Name: cmdCancel, Caption: Cancel

TextBox - Name: txtDescription, Height: 45, Width: 132, Scrollbars: 2-fmScrollbarsVertical

Label - Caption: Description:

Once you use the above commands, you should be able to see a window pop up that looks like a form.

It should have the First Name, Last Name, Department, Date, and the other commands you have entered above.

This is a simple UserForm that you can work with. You can always modify the above controls to fit your needs and create a form that works for you.

Finally, one of the things that people like to do while working with forms is to move from one section to another within the form using the TAB function. You can decide how the TAB function works.

What this means is that using specific commands, you can decide what section will the TAB function take you to next.

In order to set a specific order for your TAB command, then all you have to do is go to the View menu. Next, go ahead and select the Tab Order option. A dialog box will now open up listing all the sections of the UserForm. The order of the list dictates the order in which the TAB function works.

For example, if the order says FirstName, LastName, and the Description, then you are going to start with the First Name. When you press TAB, you will be taken to the Last Name and then if you hit TAB again, you will end up in the Description section. If you would like to change the order (for example, if you would like to go to Description after the First Name), then simply use the Move Up or Move Down buttons provided in the dialog box. This will help you perform the TAB function in the way that you would like.

TAB function becomes useful when you have to fill up the UserForm in a particular order or if you would like to change the order in which you approach the form anytime during your activity.

CHAPTER 6

Working With Conditional Statements

Macro can be used commonly to refer to macro objects, especially the ones that a user can find in the navigation window under the Macro heading. But, the reality is that several macros exist within one macro object. That is why it is referred to as a macro group. A macro group is listed as an independent macro object on the navigation window, but it is still a cluster of macros. Nevertheless, you have the freedom of creating each macro separately as an independent object, but it is not really a necessity. This is because each macro, even the ones in a group, has its own unique name for identification.

Each macro has its own individual set of actions as well. In general you will require more than one argument to perform actions for macros. As mentioned above, each macro has its own name, which you can assign to it. You can even add a number of conditions to control its actions in the application. You will find a detailed explanation of such actions in later chapters.

Note that if the macro group just has one macro listed under it, then you may not need to add separate macro names. The name of the macro group or object can then be used for referring the macro listed under it. However, macro groups with multiple macros will require particular names for each macro. If the column with the Macro name is not visible to the macro builder, then you will have to press the button for Macro Names listed under show/hide group in the tab menu for Design. Keep reading for more information about executing macros of a macro object or group.

Note that macro expansions are shortened using their macro names. And, each macro name consists of a cluster of strings that are unique. Each of these names start with a unique symbol or letter, like $, #, or @. So, macro names can be created with various symbols or alphanumeric characters as well. Often, it is recommended that you start a macro name with @ if you are using Oracle. Albeit, it is essential to have unique names to identify macros in various applications, but the global and local macros names can still be the same. In the case being discussed here, the macros in the local directory will be offered priority.

For referring to or creating a local macro with application level of control, you should use dual names, like Sample.'@JPUM'. Note that parts of a macro name with special symbols, like @, will need to be added within quotation marks (you can use double or single).

Syntax

- For local macro, the syntax is usually in this format: name1.name2
- For global macro, the syntax just needs to be: name2

The application's name is referred by name1 and the macro's name is called name2.

Arguments

With arguments, macros are provided with a value to perform an action. These actions can be about operation of specific controls, displaying of strings in a message window, etc. Many of such arguments are crucial, while others are just optional for processing.

You can find arguments in the window for Action Arguments that is under the Macro Builder menu.

The 2007 version of MS Office Access had Arguments option as a new feature. It does not let you edit the argument actions, but only view them similar to the action. With its help, a user is able to understand the macro at a much easier level, as he or she will not have to select each action separately to view the respective arguments. If you want your Excel to show the arguments menu, then you need to press the show/hide button for Arguments from the Design tab menu.

Module

If we speak with a broad perspective, a module refers to a box that is meant for VBA code. In fact, a module is the area where the written code is stored in Excel. Think of it like a cargo ship or port, where you can find stacks of containers for shipment and storage of goods, etc. Just like the cargoes are there in the real world, modules are present in the virtual world – in the case of Excel, modules contain VBA codes created for macros.

You can access the list of modules available in your workbook that you presently used in the Project Explorer. The Project Explorer is the area of the Visual Basic Editor or VBE. You can use other types of modules besides the standard ones. But, note that the standard ones are called as modules only. Modules also comprise of procedures, which will now be discussed in the next definition.

Routines And Procedures

With a procedure, which is a component of computer coding, you can perform a particular task or action. Technically speaking, a procedure is a cluster of statements that are declared with a particular statement. This declaration is ended with the End command. Note that there VBA has two types of procedures. The first one is a Sub procedure, which is used for performing actions in Excel. Plus, you can start a sub procedure with a declaration statement: “Sub.”

The second procedure is a Function, which is meant for calculations and returning values for the output. You will learn more about it later.

Statement

These are instructions that are used for commanding Excel to perform various actions. Technically, you can differentiate statements in two categories. The first one is called a declaration statement, as you read in the previous section. It can be declared by the name and is utilized for declaring a variable or a constant. The second type of statement is the one that is executable. These are responsible for specifying the exact action needed to be taken by a statement.

Another type of statement exists, which is known as Assignment statement. This statement type is used for assigning a particular expression or value to a variable or constant.

Object

The previous functions discussed above are meant for performing tasks or actions. You may ask yourself, why are these tasks being performed? The answer to it is Object. You can understand this phenomenon more clearly when you compare VBA coding with the English language. This will help you understand the logic behind the macros and VBA. Thus, let us look at English grammar to learn about an object. As per English, an object refers to an entity on which an action is performed. You can find plenty of objects in everyday life that can set as examples, like a computer, a bike, a car, etc.

Even in VBA, the situation about objects is mostly the same. This is because VBA manages and operates on the objects. Over 100 object classes are present in VBA, and this language operates various actions over all of them. Some objects that VBA influences are cells, worksheets, workbooks, cell fonts, and cell ranges. The most common objects that you will find in VBA codes for macro creation are Selection and ActiveCell. With ActiveCell, the Excel is pointing at the currently active cell, and any relevant action is going to be carried upon it in the VBA code.

On the other hand, the Selection refers to the object that has been currently selected. In a nutshell, objects are defined by their classes. Now, let us learn about classes.

Classes

As it has been explained in the above paragraph, classes are meant to define several areas of objects, including procedures, events, variables, and properties. Based on the above paragraph, you can think of objects being examples of various classes, or you can even consider them being blueprints.

As an example to explain this, think of running a business that develops motorbikes. For manufacturing a motorbike, a blueprint is going to be needed. This drawing will be needed to keep track of the design and other technicalities related to the motorbike. This motorbike blueprint is there to characterize all the features of the bike being produced at your organization. You can consider such a blueprint to be similar to classes in VBA.

With the help of a blueprint, your company can produce as many motorbikes as they want and they will not be confused about the design, features, etc. These bikes are similar to objects in VBA. Classes in Excel macros is an advanced topic that can be learned as you keep practicing the basics of Excel. Their relationship with objects is significant for sure.

Collections

VBA uses this term to refer to a group of objects. If you consider this word at the basic level, then collections are quite similar to the real world collections you know of. It is simply several objects grouped together. Furthermore, this group of objects can also be a collection if it is accurately related to each other. Thus, collections have the task of managing and grouping multiple objects together. More specifically, the ones that are related to one another.

Object Relationship With One Another

MS explains that objects have a relation with each other, as they have similarities with each other. However, the primary reason for a relationship between objects is because of the container they clustered in together. You can also refer to it as a containment relationship that lets objects with similar features being clustered together.

Another relationship exists, which you can apply to classes. This relationship is a hierarchical one. It features as such when a class is a derivation of a basic-level class.

Property

Objects comprise of various characteristics, qualities, and features, which can all be useful for getting the description of an object. With VBA, you have the ability to modify and conclude the properties related to various objects. To explain it better, here is a real life example.

Consider a dog. What do you think its properties are? It can be the size of its ears, color of its eyes or hair, etc. Besides the properties provided for this particular dog (which is an object), it will also have certain methods of its own. Let's explain that in the next section.

Methods

To explain what methods are, let us think of an example linked to English once again. It was explained earlier that an object is something upon which an action is performed. That action being performed on the object is the Method. And, Excel is performing that method or action on the object. If you recall in English grammar, something that performs an action on an object is called a Verb. So, your verb in English grammar is similar to method in VBA. In addition, let us take the dog example to learn about the components of VBA.

It was mentioned before that dogs can have methods of their own. What are they? What do you think about walking a dog? That is a method or action being performed on the object (dog) to complete an operation.

The Appearance Of Methods And Properties In Excel

In a VBA program to create macros, Excel is there to perform all the instructions that are given to it. After writing a macro code, Excel executes it and completes the commands. In any code, you will face properties, objects, and methods all clustered systematically to perform the basic action of running a macro. You will instruct Excel to perform calculations, return values, fit text in cells, change colors, shapes, etc. All these operations that you will be performing are the methods.

Arrays and Variables

In Computer Science terminology, a variable represents a location for storing a value. This storage location is given a name as well. The value is located in the memory of the machine. In fact, variables can be considered as storage areas for assigned values. Think of them as envelopes. What is the purpose of an envelope?

An envelope can be used for storing a letter, which has information in it. You can place the letter with the information in an envelope. In the case of machine language, the letter of information is similar to the value of a variable. You can even add a name on the envelope to make it more specific, just like a variable. Now, consider an instance where you want to provide someone with information that has been placed inside the envelope. Now, you have two ways of providing the person with the information related to the envelope. Either you can explain the information to the person, who will then keep opening all the envelopes to match the information that you have described.

Or, you can mention the name present on the envelope, which will help the person to choose only the specific envelope with the name you described from a cluster of envelopes. That way, the person will not have to open each and every envelope to check the information. So, what do you think is the better way to get the information from the above two methods? Surely, it is the second one, as it will consume less time.

Here is an example to explain this better:

Assume that you have dog, and now you have to take care of its diet. Assume that your dog needs eggs in its diet every day. For that, you have hired five individuals who will be feeding your dog with eggs between 5 to 10 daily. For this dietary plan to work properly, you are going to set a few rules for the hired individuals. Each person needs to feed 1 or 2 eggs to the dog.

You also instruct them to report to you and let you know the exact number of eggs they fed to the dog yesterday. Think of a VBA application to create this dietary report for your dog. In a condition where any of the individuals did not follow the instruction, which is to feed 1 or 2 eggs to the dog, then your application will send you a notification for it.

Think of this macro to be named as Dog_Eggs_Diet, where you will have to list two types of variables for this code to work. Your first variable will reflect the quantity of eggs fed by each individual to the dog. You can name this variable as "dietEggs." Your second variable is there to help with the storing of the ID number of each individual. You can name this variable as "personIdentity." Now, what is the procedure of creating the variables?

For that, you will have to declare the variable in VB editor. Upon declaring a variable, you will provide it with a name and certain characteristics. You will also instruct your Excel application to provide with a space for storing values. You can declare a variable in VBA using the Dim statement. You can find more information related to declaration statement in other chapters or sections. For now, just think of the procedure to function in this way without being confused about it.

You have the ability to declare the variable at several levels. The location where the variable is declared will show you the time when this variable will be applicable. For example, you have the choice of declaring it above the module. This variable declared at the beginning of the module will stay in memory as long as it is open. Plus, you can use these variables in all the procedures that are relevant to the modules being used.

Besides, you also have the ability of creating variables with a limited access if you declare it within a procedure and not outside a module. Such variables are limited inside the procedure in which their declaration has been made. You will be defining various variable types that store varying types of data. This can be done using the term "As." A number of variables can be used, such as Range, Boolean, String, Long, etc.

As an example for the dog diet case, the declaration of variables will be done like this:

Dim personIdentity As Integer

Dim dietEggs As Range

Now, let's understand how these statements can help with determining the track of the fed eggs to the dog. You will also understand how the variables are being used for this purpose. Note that a variable with just one value is referred to as a Scalar variable. You can use such variables when you need to consider just one item. However, in a case where you have to deal with a cluster of items related to each other, this might be difficult to utilize. In those cases, we use arrays.

Consider arrays as a cluster of elements that have the same relationship and data type linked to each of them. You can consider this function to be the same as that of a variable, which is used for holding values. The only variation is that arrays are used for several values at the same time. On the other hand one variable, or scalar variable just provides with one value.

Upon utilizing an array, your reference is based on various elements provided to the arrays that use common names. However, they are individually identified using numbers that are known as subscripts or indexes. For example, if you have a cluster of 10 dogs, and you have numbered them from one to ten, then you can call them as Dog(1), Dog(2), Dog(3), etc., until you reach at Dog(10). Now, considering the example of the dog diet code, you will now familiarize with a condition.

Condition

With the help of a condition, you are evaluating whether a statement or expression is false or true. After determining whether the expression turned out to be false or true, Excel will take the action of running the program or stopping there. This execution is carried on the statements that follow.

You can consider a condition as a statement that need to be true for an action to take place. Consider your dog diet example for coming up with a condition to follow in the code. Note that the structure for the conditional statement is in the form of If...Then. Upon observation, you will notice that you second declaration statement mentioned previously can be input with an IF...Then command. To be more precise, this is how it can be used:

If any of the individuals fail to follow the rule of not feeding 1 or 2 eggs to the dog, then your macros should notify you with a reminder. Note that conditional statements are not limited to just Excel. You can witness their usage in other programming languages as well. Based on the evaluated result, the If...Then statement will instruct Excel to follow the necessary protocol.

You can choose several ways to create your conditional statement for executing your VBA code. To give you an example of the conditional statement, please refer to the below code:

If dietEggs.Value <1 Or dietEggs.Value >2 Then

MsgBox ("You need to feed 1 or 2 eggs to the dog every day")

End If

Let us understand this snippet of code provided above. The starting code provides with two conditions that Excel will evaluate to be false or true. The code line will instruct Excel to evaluate whether the value of the dietEggs is less than one or greater than two. Note that dietEggs is determining the number of eggs fed to the dog by an individual. This is the condition where Excel concludes whether the individual has followed the rule or not.

If Excel sees that the stored value is 1 or 2, then it will know that the condition is true and it will run the second statement. If neither of the conditions are true, then it will not run the statement. If you look at the second line, you will see that it is another instruction that this snippet is providing to Excel in case either of the conditions present in the first statement is not false. In this case, if the individual has not fed any eggs to the dog or has fed more than two eggs to it, then Excel will return the message that is present in the dialogue box as a reminder. With the third code line, the If...Then statement ends.

Now, you have been familiarized with the technique of creating the variables for storing the quantity of eggs that needs to be fed to the dog daily by each of the individuals. Plus, you have also learned how Excel reminds the individuals with the message letting them know to follow the dietary rule provided. To complete this code, you will need another part that is considered as a basic function in programming structures. The following part will be helpful in understanding how each individual will be asked about the quantity of eggs they fed to the dog.

Loops

These statements are present to help carry an operation multiple times. In short, a loop is a particular statement that lets Excel follow a cluster of instruction several times. Just like the conditional statement, loops can also be structured in multiple ways. However, for the dog diet example, you will be using the For loop statement. The For loop lets Excel know to run the various statements over and over for each of the components. The loop statement can be added above the conditional statement to execute it properly.

The line of code that will be used for this particular group is given in the following way:

For Each dietEggs In Range ("B4:B8")

You can see that this statement is written in such a way to make the loop execute. You can see the representation of the elements (eggs) being discussed here by the variable dietEggs. In particular, this variable is the Range variable object. The ending part of the code talks about the group in which these elements are located. In the above situation, it is referring to the cell range from B4 cell to the B8 cell. For these sets of cells, the loop repeats the set of instructions given to it. For each loop, the conditional statement If....Then that had been discussed before is applied to fulfill the purpose.

The purpose here is to return the message if the eggs are not fed as per the condition. The loop will make sure that each individual gets a message returned to him or her upon fulfilling of the condition, regardless of being true or false. After the conditional statement, you will have to add another statement to make the loop repeat itself. For that you will use:

personIdentity = personIdentity + 1

Adding this statement will instruct Excel to move to the next individual in line and repeat the set of instructions comprising of the conditional statement again. This type of code is quite simple and can be easily understood and written. However, you can even create more complicated codes that comprise of several statements and commands, such as ExitFor or ContinueFor. These commands can help to relocate the Excel's control to specific portions of a code. The ending statement of a For loop is given by:

Next dietEggs

This statement ends the loop and lets Excel know to go to the following element, which in the case above is dietEggs.

Thus, you have been familiarized with the various functions and statements needed to learn VBA macro coding. You may have noticed that many of the terms discussed above can be used interchangeably. You can notice how all such terms work together to create a code that has a purpose to be completed. If you master all these terms, you will definitely get better at Excel macro coding.

CHAPTER 7

VBA and Macros

To understand VBA better, you need to know the difference between macros and VBA.

Difference between VBA and Macros

Note that these two are not the same, even though they have a close connection to one another. In some cases, individuals have been known to use the two terms interchangeably as well.

As mentioned above, the Visual Basic Applications is a coding language comprising of commands specifically for MS Office applications like Access, Excel, Word, and PowerPoint. On the other hand, Macros is not a coding language. In reality, macros is a just a sequence of instructions that have a very specific purpose, which is to automate various tasks in applications like Excel.

In fact, a macro is a cluster of instructions that you want Excel to perform for achieving a particular operation. With VBA, you are creating macros and not using it directly to create operations.

For example, if you have read recipe instructions, then you can consider them similar to that found in Excel macros. The aspect that you need to compare between recipe instructions and macros instructions is that they both are instructing to perform a certain set of tasks. Achieving a particular goal through such commands is the primary goal of macros.

Although the language used for instructing for recipes is in proper English, VBA has its own equivalent for macros creation. Thus, macros and VBA have a connection, but their technicality is not the exact same. However, several terms can be used within the two interchangeably.

VBA vs. Macros: Why Learn Macros?

For a long time, macros have been in development. And, their existence has been as long as that of MS Office. With macros, there is an input of DB functions that are generalized by utilizing MS access functionalities that exist. For any problems, errors, or confusions while using macros, Microsoft provides us with the Help option to resolve them. Plus, there is the Erase option that helps with the generation of macros at an easy and accomplishable level while developing them.

Furthermore, the commands and operations of the database can be implemented for generating macros in the Macros pane. You can then convert these macros into VBA for MS Access. In a majority of cases, you will just be required to make a few small edits to make the program run. All the spacing, functionality, and syntax is added to the saved file, which comprises of the VBA code. This code is specifically linked to the application for which it is being recorded. And, the best aspect of this application is that even a beginner-level programmer can understand this code and create it for running various tasks. With this process, users who are learning macros, are also able to understand about VBA code implementation.

Note that creating and recording macros is much easier compared to learning VBA programming. This is true for applications that are not that comprehensive and are present for assignments at a global level.

But, the codes that are complex will not be easy to understand for applications at an advance level.

Macros are an essential tool for those who find VBA to be harder to learn. Some options in VBA may even appear confusing at first glance for some users. But, learning and understanding them will open up new possibilities to understand this coding language. It will also help users utilize Excel, Access, etc. at a diversified level.

Learning macros may not be as time consuming as other languages, but to shorten the burden, you can target specific applications that you have to or want to use for your ease. For the ones who feel macros are tedious and time consuming, you should develop and try VBA programming for strengthening your basics. By building and learning after understanding VBA, you are able to understand how programming works. That way, you will be able to utilize them in other applications as well.

Macros will be useful for a particular set of applications only. However, as this book is dedicated to Excel Macros, then you ought to learn this coding language for improving your skills and reducing unnecessary time while computing sheets.

A couple of features that macros are known for are:

- Generating forms for multiple purposes.
- Performing loops with conditional aspects.
- Providing professional designs based on forms with interface linked to DB functions.
- Processing of background data.
- Adding modules for handling errors to help the applications run efficiently.
- Combining Word and Excel features linked to the database.

Why Is VBA Macros Worth Learning For Excel?

With Excel Macros, you are able to save a considerable amount of time for processes related to Excel or other similar applications. This frequent help offered through macros may still have a limit to it. Plus, when you are having a recording tool to work with, in this case macros, you have a high chance of committing mistakes.

With the advantage of VBA, you have the ability to comprehend your codes with better efficiency. Using VBA knowledge, you will be able to let Excel know the exact operations for running a code. This gives you the privilege of accessing more functions and capabilities. Additionally, if your usage of Excel is frequent, then learning VBA can be a plus point for you.

As mentioned earlier, Visual Basics Application is a coding language, which can be utilized with a number of Microsoft applications. While VB or Visual Basic is a coding language, VBA focuses on a specific version. Even though Microsoft has curbed the implementation of VB, VBA has gained momentum in helping various MS applications function more efficiently. Fortunately, people with little knowledge of coding, or the ones who are at a beginner level in programming, can still learn VBA due to its simple layout and user-friendly interface.

Moreover, users will get pop-up notifications and suggestions to use various commands for working using automated operations. This greatly helps in making the script codes function better. But, one needs to understand that VBA does require practice before getting used to the language. So, if VBA is a little tougher to learn than normal macros, then why would you learn it? The reason is the ability to create better codes, which is possible with VBA macros.

Instead of just pushing buttons on the workbook sheets, and letting Excel record the mouse clicks, you will have the full freedom and knowledge of using Excel macros with all its relevant capabilities and functions. But, it is essential that you know the correct way of implementing them. After regular practice, and implementing the macro codes in your spreadsheets, you will witness a decrease in the time you spend on your workbook, etc.

Furthermore, you will notice that the output predictions are much easier to comprehend, as you will be instructing Excel to execute the code in the way you want without any unclear facts. When you have developed the relevant macro using your knowledge of VBA, you will have much ease in storing the data. In fact, you will also have the ability to share it with your colleagues if you want to.

In short, the reasons to learn VBA macros in Excel is:

1. It is a beginner-level coding language.

2. It has immense practicality. You can use it for MS Office applications, including Excel.

3. It will be a great addition to your Resume.

4. It will help you sort out daunting tasks while working on Excel.

You can find many other reasons too, but for now – these should be enough to get you started with Macros.

An Example of VBA Macro coded in Excel

The best way to understand macro would be through an example. So, why not we work on an example of VBA macros to explain it better. Consider a spreadsheet that comprises of names, sales figures and store numbers where the employees are working.

With the help of the macro, the added sales figures will be inserted with their corresponding names. If you like, then you can use an online source to access VBA dialog.

```
Sub StoreSales()

Dim Sum1 As Currency
Dim Sum2 As Currency
Dim Sum3 As Currency
Dim Sum4 As Currency

For Each Cell In Range(“C2:C51”)
Cell.Activate
If IsEmpty(Cell) Then Exit For
If ActiveCell.Offset(0, -1) = 1 Then
Sum1 = Sum1 + Cell.Value
ElseIf ActiveCell.Offset(0, -1) = 2 Then
Sum2 = Sum2 + Cell.Value
ElseIf ActiveCell.Offset(0, -1) = 3 Then
Sum3 = Sum3 + Cell.Value
ElseIf ActiveCell.Offset(0, -1) = 4 Then
Sum4 = Sum4 + Cell.Value
End If
Next Cell

Range(“F2”).Value = Sum1
Range(“F3”).Value = Sum2
Range(“F4””).Value = Sum3
Range(“F5”).Value = Sum4

End Sub
```

While you may feel that this code is looking complicated, it can be segregated into parts that will then be easier for you to understand. Eventually, you will have a better grasp at the basics of VBA.

Declaring the Sub

You can notice that the module above has the syntax “”Sub.StoreSales()” at the beginning. It is the syntax to define that a new sub has been created, which is known as StoreSales. Similarly, other functions can also be defined. If you have to differentiate between a sub and a function then the basic one is that a sub cannot return a value, but a function can. This is much easier to understand if you understand basic knowledge about how programming languages are written.

Your knowledge of programming languages will also clarify that subs are simply various methods used for defining, operating, etc. without returning values. In the module above, there is no need of returning a value, so a sub has been used in it. Once the code ends, it is written “End Sub.” This instructs Excel that the VBA macro written has now been finished.

Declaring Variables

In the starting line of the program in the module, you can see the word “Dim.” This command under VBA macros is for declaring a variable. Thus, “Dim Sum1” is instructing Excel to create a new variable known as “Sum1.” Furthermore, we want Excel to know the type of variable we are looking for. So, it is essential to choose the data type as well. Several types of data exist in VBA. Through a good online source, you can locate them all.

Our example discussed above talks about currencies, so the data type used for the example is related to Currency. For that the code “Dim Sum1 As Currency” commands Excel to develop a new variable for Currency, known as “Sum1.” Every variable that has been defined, requires one statement with the term "As" to let Excel identify the type of variable or data.

Using A Loop To Start The Operation

As mentioned earlier, some knowledge of programming languages will help you easily understand loops. Nonetheless, just understand that loops are an integral part of programming languages. They help in simplifying complex codes and modules. To learn about them in depth, you can look for trustworthy online sources.

Several types of loops exist. For the above module, we are using the "For" loop. Here is how this loop type has been implemented in the code above.

For Each Cell In Range("C2:C51")

[rest of the code that follows]

Next Cell

This code is instructing Excel to use iteration for the various cells specified in the code. In the above case it is from 2nd to 51st cell of Column C. Furthermore, the example has also used the object Range, which is a particular type of object implemented with the VBA directory. Instead of specifying the action for all the cells, macros use Range to list all the cells within that range. From C2 to C51, the total number of cells this function applies to is 50.

In addition, the statement "For Each" lets Excel know that each of the cells will be applied with an operation. The statement "Next Cell" indicates that after applying a function on each cell, Excel needs to move on the next cell. With next cell, the system moves to the starting of the "For" loop. It keeps repeating the process, until all the cells within the range have been dealt with. Thus, the execution of the code goes on in a loop.

Another statement that you can find in the code is "If IsEmpty(Cell)" Then Exit For."

Many of you might be able to understand what its purpose is, as it is almost readable. For others who are confused about its function – once the cells are all finished, which means has reached a cell that does not have any values filled in it, then the loop will exit.

For your information, you can even use other loops for this code, like the "While" loop. In this case, the "While" loop would have been a better option to write this script. However, to teach you in a flow, the example used "For" loop to exit.

Using If Then Else Statement

In every code, a fundamental statement acts as the main function to execute a program. In the script above, the If-Then-Else statement is the key to this program's operation. You can find the sequence of steps listed for this below:

```
If ActiveCell.Offset(0,-1) = Then
  Sum1 = Sum1 + Cell.Value
  ElseIf ActiveCell.Offset(0, -1) = 2 Then
  Sum2 = Sum2 + Cell.Value
  ElseIf ActiveCell.Offset(0, -1) = 3 Then
  Sum3 = Sum3 + Cell.Value
  ElseIf ActiveCell.Offset(0, - 1) = 4 Then
  Sum4 = Sum4 + Cell.Value
End If
```

If you were able to understand the operation of the example above just by reading the code, then it is a good thing. It may still be possible that the statement "ActiveCell.Offset" has confused you a little bit. This statement, for example "ActiveCell.Offset(0, -1)" instructs Excel to search for the cell that is located on the left side of the active cell. The minus 1 represents a similar direction pattern as you may have known to be used in graphs. This example is letting Excel know to work on the indicated column cell for the stored number. If there is "1" located in the cell, then the value needs to be added to the value in Sum1. If Excel finds out that the value stored in the cell is "2," then it will add it to the value in Sum2 cell. This process continues in this way.

Excel will compile the complete code in this particular order working on each of the statements. Once the conditional statement has been fulfilled, then Excel moves to the "Then" statement to follow the relevant instructions. If the condition is irrelevant, then Excel takes the compilation to the next statement indicated with "ElseIf." Another case that can arise is where none of the statements were able to satisfy the condition. In that case, no action will be taken for the script.

In the program given above, the combined effort of loops and conditional statements have been helpful in fulfilling the operation for the macro. The offered loop instructs Excel to operate through each of the cells that has been chosen for fulfilling the conditions.

Writing Cell Values

The final part of the complete macro script above comprises of the results for the various conditional statements. The code for that is given below:

Range("F2").Value = Sum1

Range("F3").Value = Sum2

Range("F4").Value = Sum3

Range("F5").Value = Sum4

With the help of .Value followed by the sign for equals to, the program provides each of the cells with a value linked to its specific variable. That is how this program for the macro works. Lastly, the "End Sub" instructs Excel that the program has been completed for the Sub. That lets the application to end the VBA macro. After that, running the macro with the macro button lets you execute all the relevant additions of the sales figures in their respective columns.

Various Building Blocks Used In VBA Excel

As mentioned earlier, a complicated VBA macros can be simplified if you break it down into various parts. You will find it much more logical and easier to comprehend in small sections. Plus, once you become used to reading and writing these scripts, your subconscious mind will understand the various syntaxes for VBA macro right away!

Increase your knowledge in the vocabulary of syntaxes, codes, and statements will increase your speed in typing such macro at a much faster rate. It will also improve your logic behind the way they have to be created, resulting in better accuracy of output. Plus, it will be a much better alternative to use macros than recording clicks for creating macros.

Searching online sources for answers on various confusing parts will give you a supportive explanation of such terms and statements in detail. If you are interested in learning about these scripts in depth, then you can even Google about them. Moving to an intermediate or advance level in macros will let you perform advance-level tasks, such as looking at your PC's information, emailing through Excel, and exporting tasks in Outlook.

CHAPTER 8

Locating Macros In Excel

Before proceeding with how to use macros, it is first necessary that you understand where to find it in your Excel program. You will first have to enable it in Excel. By default, macros are always turned off. So, you will have to activate it manually.

Here is how it can be done:

1. Open Excel.
2. Click on the File tab.
3. Press the Customize Ribbon button present in the box on the left.
4. Then look for the box near the Developer section, in the extreme right in the window.
5. Press OK button to enable the Develop tab in Excel above the Ribbon.

A Tip: When you are present in the window for Customizing Ribbon, you can also remove or add items from the Excel ribbon. If you have commands that you use quite frequently, then you can add those to the Ribbon to access them quickly.

Recording and Creating Macros

To start with macros, you should first create one. Recording macros is considered the simplest way of creating macros.

Here is how it works:

Pressing the record button will prompt Excel to literally record all the future activity of button clicks you perform. Once you have completed the action, you can click on the replay button, which will cause Excel to repeat the set of clicks it recorded for you.

To be honest, you cannot find a simpler way to understand how to create macros than this in Excel. Once you have recorded a macro, you can have a look at the recorded buttons to see if you did not miss something out. If you did something wrong, then you can modify your recording, delete or add functions and combinations, and replay it to check. Note that with practice, you will be able to understand the correct way it works for you. This is just one of the ways you can learn to use macros.

But, there are several functions that are not recordable. This is a significant limitation that macros have. Recording macros is an initial step that will help you get used to the tool, but if you want to devise a more sophisticated function, then recording your steps may not be a suitable method.

For now, you need to understand this simple and useful technique to record a macro.

Ensure that you have enabled the Developer tab in your application before you start. If it is not turned on, then you can go through the previous part of this chapter to learn the steps to initiate it.

Once you have enabled the Developer tab, move on to the following steps.

1. Open a new workbook in your Excel.

2. At the bottom corner on the left, you will find an icon near the word "Ready. " Press that button to start recording the macro. The icon will change to a small square, which means that the macros is currently recording.

3. Pressing that button will open up a Record Macro window. This window has various fields to input the name, location (to store the macro in), and a shortcut key input for the macro you are recording. Either you can change the fields or leave it to default values as it is. For this example, let us leave it as default. Press OK.

4. Press the A1 cell.

5. Type the text Salesperson and press Enter

6. After that, press A2 cell and type John. Press Enter.

7. Pressing enter will take you to A3 cell, where you can type the next name say Jeremy. Press Enter again. If you made some mistake, just fix it as you usually would do and continue with the next step.

8. Once you have recorded it, you can stop the recording by pressing the square button.

Now, it is time to view your created macro.

1. Press the Developer Tab.

2. Press the first button, which says "Visual Basic." This will prompt you with a new window. This window is known as the VBA editor in Excel. Depending upon your respective settings, you may see a varying window layouts, but the options should be the same, nonetheless.

In some cases the macro may not be showing in the window, but it is right there. You just need to display it there. Before learning how to display it, let us first understand the various options on this window. The box on the upper left is known as the Project window. You will be able to notice all the worksheets of your workbook, with the modules (macros are stored in modules) that have been created.

The window on the left at the bottom is called Properties. This window displays all the properties of the object that you select in the Project window. For instance, if you select Sheet1 from the Project box, then you will be able to see its properties in the Properties window. The box on the right, which is gray in color, is the window where your macro code will be displayed.

1. Expand the modules from the Project box.
2. This will highlight the Module 1. Double click it using your mouse to show the macro on the code window.

You should be able to see the following Macro code as given below, if you followed the steps accurately.

```
Sub Macro1()

‘

‘ Macro1 Macro

Range(“A1”).Select

ActiveCell.FormulaR1C1 = “Salesperson”

Range(“A2”).Select

ActiveCell.FormulaR1C1 = “John”

Range(“A3”).Select
```

```
ActiveCell.FormulaR1C1 = "Jeremy"

End Sub
```

As per the previous information that you have been provided, you will notice that Excel chooses a cell with the help of Select method. After that, it records the value after the "=" sign for the property: FormulaR1C1. Whenever you need to input text in a particular cell, you will have to always add it within quotation marks.

The created macro will execute each code from the starting to the ending running each line that is missing a quote as the initial character.

CHAPTER 9

Locating Created Macro Codes

If you keep track of the time you spend on Excel while performing small, repetitive, and unimportant tasks, then you will understand how boring and irritating it can be. You may notice that filling up various cells in your spreadsheet, inserting, or formatting the text will take a considerable amount of time. You may a have the habit of performing these repetitive activities, and you may think that you have become quite fast in completing the task. But, it can be annoying to do so.

Think of a task where you just have to spend 5 to 10 minutes filling out every sheet with the same details about your workbook project and then sending it to clients and counterparts. Each sheet will take so much of your time just for this repetition.

In most of the cases, you are going to not yield any productive results out of this activity. In fact, this situation in Excel is considered to be a major example in unproductive and repetitive approach. While going through this book, you must feel the importance and power of macros to help you get over such repetitions. With their help, you will be free from typing and filling everything again and again.

Thus, you chose this guide and now, it will help you with performing the tasks and learning the basics of macros. Creating macros will now be discussed within this chapter.

You have been introduced to setting up macros in one of the previous chapters. Now, it is time to learn how to find them.

Location of Macro Code

As mentioned earlier, the Project Window will help in navigating various modules, functions, etc. On expanding VBA Project window, you will see two folders: one is related to Modules, and the other is for Objects in Excel. You can find various elements provided to you in the Objects folder. But, the elements will not be present in the Modules folder. Click on the plus sign next to the Modules folder to check its contents.

The components that are present in the Objects folder may feel familiar to you, but you may still feel a little confused about a Module folder and its components. In simple words, you can consider a module to be a folder for VBA program. All the codes that are written in VBA are stored in the Module folder. Upon recording a macro, you will find that its code gets stored in the module folder under the name Module1.

To view this VBA code, you just have to right click the Module1 component or double click it to view the recorded macro code. This will display the VBE macro code in the coding window present next to it. When you look at the displayed code, do you feel it is making any sense? Some parts that are mostly in English will make sense to you. However, other parts may still feel confusing to you. Another query that may come to your mind while going through the code is that why such instances such as changing the color of fonts, fitting columns automatically, changing color of cells, writing text, etc. requires such complicated programming? This question is a common one that many non-programmers have in their minds. The following section will help you understand the reason for that.

Implementing Excel Macro Code For Learning VBA From The Fundamental Level

A positive sign that you can agree to while learning macro code is that it somewhat resembles the English language. To make it easier for users to code in VBA, the use of structured English is relevant, which is quite similar to the common English we speak. The use of English words structured for certain operations is a key strategy that helps in understanding the instructions in an efficient way. This way, not only Excel, but the user who is typing the code is able to understand what the command is meant to perform in VBA. Understanding some words and instructions will also help keep track of what the program is meant to do at a complex level.

That does not mean that all programming languages are comprising of English words that make sense for the user. Some languages have specific syntaxes that are not easy to understand despite being in English. VBA, on the other hand, still is an easier coding language that gives a fundamental knowledge of how programming languages work for beginners.

Here is a small example of VBA code:

Sub Easy_Excel_Tutorial()

‘

‘ Easy _Excel_Tutorial Macro

‘ Types “This is an easy Excel tutorial”. Auto-fits column. Cell color red. Font color blue.

‘

```
' Keyboard Shortcut: Ctrl+Shift+B
'
        ActiveCell.Select
        ActiveCell.FormulaR1C1 = "This is an easy Excel tutorial"
        Selection.Columns.Autofit
        With Selection.Interior
                .Pattern = xlSolid
                .PatternColorIndex = xlAutomatic
                .Color = 255
                .TintAndShade = 0
                .PatternTintAndShade = 0
        End With
        With Selection.Font
                .Color = -4165632
                .TintAndShade = 0
        End With
End Sub
```

After going through the above code, you may want to understand certain terms used in it that may or may not be confusing.

ActiveCell.Select:

This command is meant to point out to the cells that are actively selected in your worksheet. Any beginner will be able to fathom the use of the word "Select" in Excel or VBA. You can understand that this word represents choosing a particular selection. In this case, we are choosing an active cell.

Selection.Columns.Autofit:

Another simple command that has a clear purpose of selecting the columns and fitting them automatically based on their width. Any text that has been typed in the cells of this column will be symmetrically adjusted for creating a more prominent and good-looking column in the worksheet. The text typed in the cell will be completely visible and adjusted within it.

Note that such terms and commands will be frequently dealt with while you learn macro code. So, you need to understand its fundamentals.

The Fundamentals oF Excel Macro Code

To understand it better, we will now go through the complete code example given above. You need to examine it line by line to learn how Excel runs the macro. Even if you are not able to understand some or all of the lines in the program, you do not have to worry for now. The objective here is to help you understand the basics of the VBA macro code and its operations. Plus, it will show how Excel will follow the instructions step by step to change the color of the font, color of the active cell, and write the line instructed in the program.

Another thing that you will notice in the created macro is that the code incorporates various actions that you did not actively carry out. Do not worry about the lines that may appear useless at that instance, as the actions given to Excel will be translated into code eventually for it to process.

For now, let us understand the various parts of the programming code written:

1. Sub Easy_Excel_Tutorial()

The expression Sub present in this line of code is the short form for Sub Procedure. It is a type of procedure that you can utilize for developing codes in Excel macros. There are two types of procedures, and this is one of them. With sub procedures, you are instructing Excel to carry actions or activities within it. Besides Sub, the other procedure is Function. As mentioned in one of the previous chapters, the Function is helpful in returning a value or performing calculations.

Thus, with the code above, you are instructing Excel to create a Sub. To create such type of a procedure, you always have to start with the word Sub, after which the name of the procedure is added, followed by parentheses. At the end, the sub needs to be completed using the command “End Sub.”

2. The lines followed by an apostrophe

You can see the lines that are given followed by an apostrophe (‘). These refer to as comments and have the following features:

- You indicate comments using the apostrophe, so they start after the symbol (‘).

- Any line that follows this symbol is ignored by VBA until the end. While executing the code, such lines will not be compiled by Excel.

- Based on the previous action, the primary reason for comments in a code is to help the user get some information relevant to the macro code. This way, it is easier to understand what the code is about. With comments, developers share information among themselves to clear the purpose of a particular code. Moreover, any recent modifications that have been made in the code are also referenced using comments. Almost all programming languages have their own ways of highlighting comments in codes to explain procedures better.

3. ActiveCell.Select

Just like the first line of code explained before, this one also selects an active cell in Excel. To be more precise:

- The current cell active in the sheet's active window is the ActiveCell.
- With select, the object becomes active on the current worksheet. The ActiveCell is the cell that is currently active in this one.

4. ActiveCell.FormulaR1C1 = "This is an easy Excel tutorial"

This statement is instructing Excel to write the line in the currently active cell. Let us check the various parts of this line one by one. By now, you have already understood the reason for ActiveCell to be there in the line. The part written as "FormulaR1C1" is there to instruct Excel for setting up a formula for the object. For the code above, the formula will be set up for the active cell.

The code R1C1 is indicating a relative cell, instead of an absolute cell. You will find more details about R1C1 later. Understand that recording a macros in this case is a relative one, which can have a varying active cell, instead of a fixed one. The formula to which this code is referring to in this case is the text "This is an easy Excel tutorial." This case wants the text to be filled in the currently active cell or the object.

5. Selection.Columns.AutoFit

As explained earlier, the columns will be auto-fitted using this command in the active cell. This will fit the complete text in the cell with the help of the command. The purpose of the various parts used in this command will now be explained:

- Selection: This is referring to the present selection. In the current case, it is referring to the active cell.

- Columns: This is referring to the columns selected using the command. In this case, the column with the active cell is bring referred here.

- AutoFit: You can understand the purpose of this word easily. The command automatically adjusts the width of the column selected with the active cell. Autofit is not just limited to columns, but also to rows. So a relevant code with rows in selection can also be used for serving the macro code purpose.

6. The Code From With … to End With

Until now, the macro code statements discussed above are performing the two functions that it had been programmed to do, which are: filling the text "This is an easy Excel Tutorial" in the active cell, and auto-fitting it in the active cell of the column. Now, the code that starts with "With" instructs Excel to perform the next set of instructions.

These comprise of changing the color of the active cell to red. It may feel that changing the color of an active cell is a simple step, but in as per the programming limitations, this is a multi-step procedure to perform. To perform this coloring operation, you will have to use the statement With…End With.

The primary objective of this statement is to create a simple syntax for running a particular set of instructions for the same object at every instance. For this particular code, the object being referred to is the active cell. You can see in the main code above that there are two With – End With command statements, which are both serving their respective purposes.

These statements comprise of the structure below:

The code needs to start with the syntax referring to the objectExpression. So it becomes "With objectExpression." For now, you do not need to understand much about the term objectExpression. Think of it as a typename variable that is replaced with selection. In this case, "Selection.Interior" is the objectExpression for the first statement for With-End With.

Similarly, "Selection.Font" is the objectExpression for the next statement. These code or set of codes are mentioned in the created macro so that Excel can execute it by referring to the selected object. With the help of the "With" statement, you are instructing Excel to follow the necessary protocol. Later, the code is ended with the "End With" statement.

From the code you can understand the part within the first With…End With syntax. For your understanding, here is the code being referred to once again:

```
With Selection.Interior

        .Pattern = xlSolid

        .PatternColorIndex = xlAutomatic

        .Color = 255

        .TintAndShade = 0

        .PatternTintAndShade = 0

End With
```

Based on the above code, we will now explain each of these line one after the other.

- **The First Line:** This line is instructing Excel to refer to the active cell's interior while running the various statements. These statements are within the With-End With statement. To perform this action, a user needs to start with the "With" command, like done in the code above. This code commands Excel that the lines of code that follow after the With syntax need to be executed.

  The Selection in "Selection.Interior" refers to selecting the active cell, as explained previously. The term Interior here refers to the object's interior. In this case is the active cell's interior. As mentioned earlier, "Selection.Interior" together are referred to as an objectExpression.

- **The Second Line (Pattern = xlSolid):** This line is the first one after the starting of the With-End With command. It has been added in reference to the interior of the currently active cell. With it, the code is setting a color pattern for the interior of the active cell so that it does not choose solid colors. You can accomplish this by this:

  1. "Pattern" will help in setting up the pattern inside the cell.
  2. "xlSolid" will help in marking so that the pattern is solid color.

- **The Third Line (PatternColorIndex = xlAutomatic):** With this command line, you are adding an automatic pattern for the active cell's inner portion. This is how the parts function:

  1. "PatternColorIndex" will help in setting the inner pattern's color.

2. "xlAutomatic" is used for ensuring that the color is selected automatically.

- **The Fourth Line (.Color = 25):** With this statement, you are instructing Excel to select the color that is needed for filling up the inner part of the active cell. The term "Color" is there for assigning the color for the cell. Since the number 25 has been added beforehand, so this makes the choice absolute, which in this case is the color red.

- **The Fifth Line (.TintAndShade = 0):** With this line of code, you are instructing Excel to choose a color that is neither too light nor dark for filling the interior of the active cell. The command ".TintAndShade" is being used for making a decision for the color to lighten or darken it appropriately for the active cell. In this case, the value for this command has been set as zero, which sets a neutral color for the cell. So, there is no lightening or darkening in the chosen cell.

- **The Sixth Line (.PatternTintAndShade = 0):** Just like before, this command is also set for choosing the color for the pattern in the interior of the active cell. Being set to zero, the pattern color chosen will not be a shade or tint for the interiors of the active cell. With the ".PatternTintAndShade" command, the decision for the shade and tint pattern will be made for the selected cell.

- **The Seventh Line (End With):** As discussed before, this line will instruct Excel that the With---End With statement has now ended.

7. The Second With-End With Statement

You have already learned about the operation of the With-End With statement in the previous steps. The code provided does have two such statements, so now the second With-End With statement will be discussed. As you have judged by now, this statement is performing the relevant action to create the macros. The action that it is executing is of changing the color of the font to blue. You can also see that this statement is a lot shorter than the first one. Based on the general structure it displays, each line will now be explained.

- **The First Line (With Selection.Font.):** It starts by opening the statement with the With command, which provides Excel with instructions to follow the subsequent statements for the defined object appearing there. The object being discussed in the statement is "Selection.Font." As per previous discussions, Selection is the current choice for the written macro code. This choice of object being mentioned in the statement is the active cell. Furthermore, the Font refers to the font of the text in the active cell. Thus, "Selection.Font" is indicating the active cell's text font. With the "With Selection.Font" command, Excel is following the necessary instructions on the active cell text font.

- **The Second Line (.Color = -4165632):** This particular line of code is also instructing Excel about the color of choice. In this case the color chosen is an absolute color, as the relevant value for the color has been provided in the macro. The code represents the blue color, which will be chosen for the text font in the active cell.

- **The Third Line (TintAndShade = 0):** This statement is also similar to the one in the previous With-End With command. With it, Excel will keep a neutral color for the chosen shade, which is neither light nor dark. With the "TintAndShade" command, the lightening or darkening can be changed. But, the value given is zero, which makes the shade a neutral color, which means it does not lightens nor darkens for the active cell text font.

- **The Fourth Line (End With):** Just like before, this statement ends the With statement. Thus, any code that follows this statement is irrelevant to the With-End With command.

8. EndSub

This statement marks the end of the sub procedure chosen for this particular macro code. As soon as Excel compiles this statement, it is instructed that the macro has now terminated. Beyond this statement, no line of code exists to be executed.

Useful Tips For Understanding Macros

If you really feel like learning macros in Excel at a faster pace, then these tips will definitely help you to improve your efficiency and speed. For understanding these tips better, you can use the code example mentioned in the previous section of this chapter as a reference.

- **Tip 1: Modify various VBA macro code portions to keep learning new aspects:**

  As an example for this tip, you can modify the statement "ActiveCell.FormulaR1C1 = "This is an easy Excel tutorial" and change it to "ActiveCell.FormulaR1C1 = "MS Excel is easy!" You will see that the statement being filled in the active cell, as per the code will now change to the new text.

  Similarly, you can also experiment with the colors selected for the font and interior of the active cell. For example, change the value of the color from 255 to 155 and the other color value from -4165632 to 185. You can see the changes in the colors yourself.

- **Tip 2: Try removing some of the statements from the code to see how it influences the complete macro:**

As an example, what changes might occur if you remove the statement: “Selection.Columns.AutoFit”? Surely, your text in the column’s active cell will not be completely fitted within the cell. You can have a look at such changes by running the Excel macros again after modifying it. Just use the short cut key combination: “Ctrl + Shift + B” and have a look at the result yourself. You will find that the changes made using the above two tips will alter the result you had from the previous macro code. Thus, modifying like this will help you understand how the code works more efficiently.

- **Tip 3: Keep repeating and practicing the steps that you learn:**

  Mastering macros is the easiest when you practice it regularly. Repeating your exercises, and practicing new codes will give you the upper hand in understand how it functions. Make sure you follow the example provided in the previous section. Do look for more such examples through various sources and study how each of the command function to modify the worksheet. A good way of practicing is by keeping a real time view of the editor screen beside your code window so that you can see the changes made through your macro code there only. You may need a dual-monitor setup for maximum efficiency in this case.

- **Tip 4: Keep studying for it and read various sources:**

  Find genuine sources that teach you about Excel macros besides this book. Note that this book is covering a basic understanding of how macros work. For practicing exercises and examples, you can register yourself on authentic web portals that are dedicated to Excel macros. You can even join forums supporting this coding language to ask your queries whenever you have while practicing.

CHAPTER 10

Optimization Of VBA Code For Quicker Approach To Macros

This chapter will cover the improvement and optimization introduction and techniques for you to practice. These practical techniques are great to strengthen your basics as a VBA programmer. Moreover, you can easily be counted among expert programmers if you are capable of optimizing your macro code.

With optimized VBA codes, you are saving a lot of your time, which is why you will now learn various ways of optimizing your code. Note that, you will have to understand each of the following methods religiously and implement them in your programming to create automation, dashboards, and Excel reports.

1. Logic Analyzation

Planning to optimize your code before even understanding the logic behind it is a bad move. So, you need to first understand why you are performing such an action on your macro. Without the relevant logic behind it, there may never be a significant value added to a written VBA program. Streamlining a code requires a logic behind it, which in return will offer you a high-performing macro.

2. Switch off the updating screen

You should avoid repainting or flickering of your screen, which can be bothersome while working on a code. You can do this with the following code:

> *Application.ScreenUpdating = False* 'This will switch off the updating at the starting of your code.

> *Application.ScreenUpdating = False* 'This will switch on the updating after the code has ended.

3. Switch of the calculations carried out automatically

When there is a change in the number or content of the currently active cell, the formulae assigned to such a cell will also change. This results in high volatility in the calculations in the cell, as the complete data starts recalculating automatically. It can result in a lower performance, as you may not need the data to be calculated at that moment. For that, you can turn of the calculations being carried out using the following code:

> *Appllication.Calculation = xlCalculationManual* ' This will switch of the calculations at the starting of the code.

> *Application.Calculation = xlCalculationAutomatic* ' This will switch the calculation back on after the code ends.

After that, when you need to implement the logic of the program to calculate the data using the formulae (as the macros is dependent on the formulae), you will need to implement the code below:

> *ActiceSheet.Calculate* ' This will calculate the filled formulae in the currently active worksheet.

> *Application.Calculate* ' This will calculate the data using the formulae for all the workbooks currently active in Excel.

4. Disabling the Events

You can use the following code to stop the events from reducing the performance of the macros.

Application.EnableEvents

You can instruct the processor of the VBA language to fire the events. As there is a rare chance of firing of events during the modification of a code, you may not need it active at the moment. So, it is better to turn them off and increase the performance of the macro code.

5. Hiding the page breaks

When you are using the latest MS Excel version to execute the VBA macros, it may take longer to execute than normal. This will cause them to take more time than the previous versions of Excel. In fact, the macros that need several seconds to accomplish a task in the previous versions of Excel will need several minutes to fulfill in the latest versions. This can occur when some of the conditions become active. To make it run more efficiently, you can disable the page breaks that occur while writing the code. This can be done using:

ActiveSheet.DisplayPageBreaks = False

6. Utilizing the "With" command while processing objects

When a user is trying to retrieve the methods and properties of an object within multiple lines of code, he or she will have to avoid using the name of the object. Plus, he or she will also have to avoid utilizing the complete path of the object over and over. This can cause the VBA processor to reduce in performance as it has to use complete compilation for the object every time it runs through it. This is similar to what macros have been designed to do. Think of a user who has to perform the same task repeatedly. Your VBA program may also not like this action. Thus, we use "With" statement to make things faster.

Here is an example of a slow and fast macro covering the With statement.

Example of a Slow Macro:

Sheets(1).Range("A1:E1").Font.Italic = True

Sheets(1).Range("A1:E1").Font.Interior.Color = vbRed

Sheets(1).Range("A1:E1").MergeCells = True

Example of a Fast Macro:

```
With Sheets(1).Range("A1:E1").Font.Italic = True

.Font.Interior.Color = vbRed

.MergeCells = True

End With
```

The importance of understanding the two macro codes is that, while both perform the same task, the faster macro is using the "With" statement. This statement engages in minimum object qualification for the code. This increases the performance of the code as there is less data to be compiled in it. With this statement, you do not have to write the complete concept comprising of Range, etc.

7. Instead of dual double quotes, you should use vbNullString

This command is a little faster compared to the use of double quotes. This is because vbNullString acts as a constant that has zero bytes of memory. On the other hand, double quotes is a string that has a memory of 4 – 6 bytes, that can cause a little more processing while dealing with a macros. For example:

Instead of using *strVariable = ""* , you can use *strVariable = vbNullString*.

8. Free the object variable memory they are using

When an object is created in a macro code, the program creates two memories for it. These are a pointer and an object. The pointer is also called as a reference for the object. You may hear it from experts that VB does not require pointers, but it is not the case. The truth is that VB uses pointers but does not allow a user to change them. At the backend, the program keeps using pointers as well.

To remove the object in Visual Basic, you can change its value as null. However, this arises a question: If the program is continuously utilizing object pointers, how can its value be changed to null? The answer to it cannot be removed. Upon setting the pointer value to null, a process known as garbage collector comes into play. This program chooses to destroy the object or leave it be. You can authorize this garbage collector in multiple ways. However, VB utilizes a way known as Pointer count method. In this process, once Visual Basic is done analyzing the last line of code where the object is set to null, it moves the pointer that is existing. At that particular time, there are no assigned pointers to that object. At that moment, the garbage collector removes the object and destroys all its active resources. If, however, there is a pointer referencing to the same object, it will not be removed.

9. Reduce the number of lines with the help of colon (:)

It is prudent to avoid using multiple statements individually, when you can still join them together to create a single line. You can understand this by the following examples:

Example of Slow Macro:

With Selection.WrapText = True

.ShrinkToFit = False

End With

Example of Fast Macro:

With Selection.WrapText = True:.ShrinkToFit = False

End With

As you can witness from the examples given above, several statements can be joined together when you use the colon symbol. After implementing it in the code, you can witness a reduction in the readability as well as the speed for the written code.

For the faster code, the logic behind it that is compiled is:

Upon saving the macro, it is compiled digitally. Compared to the one that is readable by a human and found in the VB editor, the keywords used take up a token of 3 byte. You cannot use keywords as variables. Plus, keywords process at a much faster rate as these are understood by the computer much better. The literal strings, variables, and comments on the contrary are not directives or keywords. These are saved in the code as they are. A VBA compiling tool will tokenize the words, but will not do the same to the lines. Plus, these lines are not shortened and stays as they are. These also end with a carriage return (meaning resetting the position of the line of code).

Upon execution of a VBA macro, the processor compiles each line one at a time. Each token of the line being compiled is then saved with the help of digital compilers. Then the processes of interpretation and execution follow. After that, the process moves on to the next line after it. With the use of a colon to join several lines into one, there is a reduction in the processes occurring to fetch the data by the VBA program, thus improving speed and performance.

The modification will end up improving the code. Moreover, there is a limit of using just 255 characters in one line. You may not have an efficient debugging process with the help of F8 key. Thus, it is not advisable to write long single lines, just to make the code more readable, which will only sacrifice the speed and performance.

10. Declaring multiple constants as Constant and several variables as Variable

It may seem a pretty obvious tip to utilize in your code, but many users do not follow this. For instance:

```
Dim Pi As Double

Pi = 3.14159
```

Instead of this, you can use,

```
Const Pi As Double

Pi = 3.14159
```

As the value of Pi does not change, its evaluation will be processed during the compiling process, which is unlike the processing of other variables. Other variables require processing multiple times.

11. Do not Copy Paste codes Unnecessarily

Copying and pasting codes can be bad for a code's performance. You can optimize your code without the need of copy pasting various steps with the following tips:

Avoid this:

```
Sheet1.Range("A1:A200").CopySheet2.Range("B1").PasteSpecial

Application.CutCopyMode = False    'Clear Cliboard
```

Instead, use this:

'Bypassing the clipboard

Sheet1.Range("A1:A200").CopyDestination: =
Sheet2.Range("B1")

Avoid This:

Sheet1.Range("A1:A200").CopySheet2.Range("B1").PasteS pecialxlPasteValues

Application.CutCopyMode = False 'Clear Cliboard

Instead, Use this:

'Bypassing the clipboard, if there is a need for only values

Sheet2.Range("B1:B200").Value =
Sheet1.Range("A1:A200").Value

Avoid This:

Sheet1.Range("A1:A200").CopySheet2.Range("B1").PasteS pecialxlPasteFormulas

Application.CutCopyMode = False 'Clear Cliboard

Instead, use this:

'Bypassing the clipboard, if there is a need of formulas

Sheet2.Range("B1:B200").Formula =
Sheet1.Range("A1:A200").Formula

'You can apply a similar code with Array formulas and FormulaR1C1.

12. Utilizing the functions in the worksheets instead of creating your own logic

While it may seem logical to develop and use something that the user understands better, it may not be the case for Excel as well. It is always prudent to use the native codes provided in the worksheet so that the code can be processed at a much faster rate. Using *Application.WorkSheetFunction* is instructing the VBA processor to utilize the codes present natively in the function sheet instead of the interpreted ones. Your Visual Basic Application will have an easier time understanding the code that is already present in the sheets for it to use.

Here is an example for it:

```
mProduct

Application.WorksheetFunction.Product(Range("C7:C14"))
```

Rather than using your own logic to define the code, like:

```
mProduct = 1

For i = 7 to 14

mProduct = mProduct * Cells(4,i)

Next
```

13. Replace statements like "Indexed For" with "For Each"

When a code is involving a looping sequence, you should avoid using the statement "Indexed For". Here is an example of the modification of the above code to explain this:

```
For Each myCel in Range("C7:C14")

mProduct = mProduct * myCell.Value

Next
```

This is related to the qualification of objects and works in a similar way as a "With" statement.

14. Avoid using "Macro Recorder" similar to a code

Using this code will help in improving performance of your macro. Here is an example to explain it better:

Avoid this:

Range("A1").Select

Selection.Interior.Color = vbRed

Instead, use this:

[A1].Interior.Color = vbRed

Peppering your code with statements like "Selection" and "Select" is going to cause reduction in performance for your macro. You need to understand the reason behind going to cell and modifying its properties, when you can simply use the latter command to change it there only.

15. Do not use variants and objects in the statement of declaration

After focusing on a prudent logic, make sure you are avoiding the use of variants and objects in the declaration statements. For instance:

Avoid using:

Dim mCell As Object or

Dim i As Variant

By specifying the type or value of a variable, you are helping the macro save extra memory. This can have a greater benefit when dealing with objects that are larger in size. It can be confusing to remember the exact entity that you had declared as a variant. This can result in misusing the variable when the value is being assigned to it. In fact, Excel might typecast it without showing any syntax errors.

Furthermore, the descriptor for the variant is 16 bytes in length, the integer is 2 bytes in length, long is 4 bytes in length, and double is 8 bytes in length. Misusing these can have a drastic impact on the code's performance. Instead, you can use:

Dim I As Long

Instead of

Dim I As Variant

Similarly:

Avoid using:

Dim mCell As Object 'or

Dim mSheet As Object

Instead, use:

Dim mCell As Range 'or

Dim mSheet As Worksheet

16. Direct Declaration of OLE Objects

Declaring and defining Object Linking and Embedding (OLE) objects in the statement of declaration is known as "Early Binding." On the other hand, declaring and defining objects is known as "Late

Binding." Note that it is always prudent to choose Early Binding over Late one. For example:

Avoid using:

Dim oXL As Object

Set oXL = CreateObject("Excel.Application")

Instead, use:

Dim oXL As Excel.Application

CHAPTER 11

Tips And Shortcuts For Excel Macros And VBA Codes

Macros Keyboard Shortcut Assignment

In this chapter, let us take into view 2 varying ways for developing keyboard shortcuts to execute macros. In addition, you will also learn about the pros and cons of both the methods for shortcut keys.

With the assignment of keyboard shortcuts, you are reducing the time it take to type the code and process it during its execution in Excel. This is generally applicable when there is a need to perform various actions in repetition. In this chapter, you will see how the two methods will use the shortcut keys to utilize the speed and efficiency of the program. These two ways will now be discussed one by one.

The First Method: The Window For Macro Options:

With the help of the macro options window, you can create shortcut keys for running various macros from time to time. You can find the instruction to set these up below:

1. You can start this by finding the Develop tab option and then pressing the button highlighted as macros. You can check the instructions provided in one of the previous chapters to enable your Developer tab option if it is not visible in the Ribbon.

You can also use the short key combination: Alt + F8 for enabling the Developer tab.

2. Upon choosing the macro to which you are looking to assign the shortcut key, press the Options button.

3. In the pop-up window for Macros Options, you can create the shortcut you want to add for it by pressing a number, symbol, or a letter. You need to beware of not overriding the shortcuts that existing beforehand. Some shortcuts are already existing, like Ctrl + V for pasting. To avoid overriding any existing shortcut keys, you can join your selected number, symbol, or letter with a shift key as well. This will make the combination a little complex, but it will not be overridden. So, the code can become Ctrl + Shift + V.

To delete an existing shortcut key, you need to first access the Macro options window just like in the previous steps. After that, you just have the delete the symbol, letter, or number assigned in the box there.

The Second Method: Application.OnKey The VBA Method:

With the help of VBA code, you can create shortcuts for your macros. The statement that you can use for this is the "Application.OnKey." This statement can help in removing and creating shortcuts. Plus, it will feature a number of options, which are more flexible than the macro option method. You need to first start it by using the Visual Basic editor. For this, just press the VB button of the Developer option tab. You can also use the shortcut key combination: Alt + F11.

Using OnKey to create shortcuts

In this technique using VB editor, a code will be written to assign the keyboard shortcuts to their respective macros.

First, you will need to develop a macro and name it properly, such as CreateShortcut. After that, you will then begin a new line with the command statement "Application.OnKey." This statement will follow a space. Note that there are two parameters in the Application.OnKey technique. The first one is for the procedure, and the second one is for the key.

Here, the key is the shortcut key combination on the keyboard. On the other hand, the procedure is macro name that is called upon typing the key combination. You need to enclose both parameters within quotes.

Check out this example to learn it better:

Sub CreateShortcut() 'Name of the macro

Application.OnKey "+^{V}", "CellColorBlue" 'This happens when you press the combination later while running the macro

End Sub

In the above example, you can see that the combination shortcut has been described as "+^{C}". This is the key parameter being used in the macro code. Note that + sign is code that is used for Ctrl, and ^sign is used for Shift. Plus, V is the key that has been added in braces. You can find the complete list of codes for all the key combinations through online sources. Using this code, you are naming the procedure and assigning it to the relevant key combination. The above code example is using the key combination to execute a macro known as "CellColorBlue."

Deleting key combination shortcuts with the help of OnKey

For this check out the code first:

Sub DeleteShortcut()

Application.OnKey "+^{V}"

End Sub

You can figure out that the code used for deleting the shortcut key is easy. It looks quite similar, with little modification to the one for creating the key combination. Instead of adding “CreateShortcut”, this code adds “DeleteShortcut”. Plus, you can notice that the name of the procedure has also been removed. Removing it is instructing Excel that there is no need to assign any combination strokes on the keyboard to perform an action. Plus, it is a command that is resetting the combinations on the keyboard to their default setting in Excel. For example, if you use the Ctrl + V combination, it will process the computer to perform a pasting action when the keys are pressed.

The techniques for deleting and creating macros have several code lines when utilizing the OnKey technique. It will let you assign shortcuts for various macros and that too all at once.

Using automatic OnKey setup with events:

Such processes of assigning shortcut key combinations can also be automated using the events Workbook_BeforeClose and Workbook_Open. You can do that with the help of the following instructions:

1. Find the Project Window in the Visual BasIC Editor window, and double click to open an existing workbook.

2. Choose the Workbook from the menu dropping down.

3. It will include the event Workbook_Open. After that, add the code line for a created macro. For this, let’s assume that the code for calling the macro is “CallModule1.CreateShortcut”. Note that the code will not have the quotes. In addition, you can even delete the macro by adding another event for closing the workbook at any instance. For that, you need to choose BeforeClose from the drop-down option present on the right-hand side of the window. After that you can call the macro.

If the storage of the macros is in a personal workbook, you can stick to the same procedure as discussed in the previous steps. You can look for online sources to study the creation of a personal workbook for macro. You can also learn about the advantages they have.

The Pros And Cons Of The Two Methods

For the two methods, you can utilize keyboard shortcuts for each file that you open in Excel. This is true for the time the file that has the macro stays open. Here is a list of the pros and cons for both the methods now:

Pros of Macro Options Window:

Setting up the keyboard shortcuts using macro options is quite easy. For the ones who feel that writing a program to create a macro shortcut is tough, this method is a boon.

Cons of Macro Options:

1. Several limitations exist when it comes to the usage of keys or key combinations. Some keys that cannot be used for shortcuts are Page Up, End, Home, etc.

2. Another issue that can arise in Macro options method is that a key may already be assigned to another shortcut. So, if you are a developer, your assigned key combinations may not control the execution of certain tasks that the user processes. Assigning key and overriding them may create confusions for the user and the developer. Plus, the order of operation for the macro names is alphabetically. This is because the macro names present in the open workbooks are present on the computer of the user.

3. No index exists for the shortcut keys using this method. You cannot look at them in a specific directory or archive. Thus, if you have already created several of them and you cannot keep

track of them, then it can be difficult for you to use them. You do have macros that can help you keep track of the created shortcuts, but that will only consume more time for you to prepare one.

Pros Of Application.OnKey Technique:

1. It is easier to find a keyboard shortcut with the help of a VBA code with the keyword OnKey. You can implement the use of the Ctrl + F combination that will open the find window for searching in the Visual Basic Editor.

2. If several macros or workbooks are using the same shortcuts, you may order or prioritize the executing macros. The shortcuts that are developed with the help of the OnKey technique are prioritized compared to the ones that are created using Macro Options. Thus, executing the technique using OnKey will ensure that the shortcut key created using it is run before other options.

3. You can use the delete or remove action with much ease for keyboard shortcuts in this method. You may have to create macro keys for disabling and enabling them from the Ribbon using the keyboard. Another way of doing so is by using one shortcut on the keyboard to toggle multiple shortcuts on the keyboard.

4. You can also use certain special buttons that may not be usable in the Macro options method. These buttons include Page Down, End, Alt, Home, etc. In addition, the combined keys Alt + Ctrl will offer various options for shortcut keys.

5. Depending on the various workbook conditions, the shortcuts can modify the procedures dynamically.

Cons of Application.OnKey Technique

1. With a modification in the macro name, the code will also need to be revised.

2. You will have to be present to process the action for the assignment of shortcuts and execute them.

Thus, you have been briefed about the two methods for assigning shortcuts for macros. Which method do you think is more suitable for you? Surely, any expert developer who uses macros is going to choose the OnKey technique as it is more efficient in multiple ways. Plus, it offers the ability to find the shortcuts in a much easier way. It also has more options for the key combinations, and has a decent control over disabling and enabling the shortcut keys (even for multiple shortcuts at once using toggle macro).

But, note that even this method is flawed in some ways. So, there is no perfect method, and you will have to decide for yourself to choose the one that makes you most comfortable. Nevertheless, try to master the OnKey method as it will give you better benefits than Macro options method.

Some Important Excel Macros Shortcuts That You Can Learn

Now, we will go through some shortcuts and tips that you can utilize in your Excel workbooks for saving time. Using these for macros and other applications related to MS Office will give you a head start while working. Note that this section will discuss some of those shortcuts and tips to help you out, but that does not mean that these are the only ones. You can find more through online research for VBA and Macros shortcuts.

That said, let us start:

1. **Alt + F11 (Opens the VBE window):** The editor window for Visual Basic or VBE can be opened using this shortcut key. As

you already know, VBE is used for creating forms for users and writing macros. You can also click the Visual Basic button present in the Developer Tab option in Excel. Choosing the shortcut key is faster and more efficient. Similarly, you can use a similar combination key for Mac PCs. But, the only change is that the key combination has an Opt instead of Alt. So, the key shortcut is Fn + Opt + F11 or Opt + F11. For enabling the Developer tab option in your Ribbon, you can look for the instructions discussed in one of the previous sections of this book.

2. **Ctrl + Space (completes words automatically):** This key action is one of the most widely used among developers of VBA. While using the codes, the Ctrl + Space key combination will open a dropdown menu that incorporates constants, variables, properties, methods, and objects.

   In addition, you can implement the Ctrl_Space shortcut using your Visual Basic editor as well. For that you can do the following:

   - Start by typing a code statement, like ActiveCell.
   - Once you type the first few keys, press the Ctrl + Space keys.
   - You will see a dropdown for a group of all the words in VBA that start with the word Act.
   - You can use the down and up arrow keys to choose the word you want to use.
   - After that you can press Enter or Tab to select the word and complete it automatically.

   You get two important pros with this shortcut key. Besides being great supporters in saving your time while you are using the debug action for your codes, these will:

- Save time for you without the need of typing long variables or words.
- Curb any chances of unnecessary typos while typing the code.

3. **The Function Keys On Laptops:** If you have been using a keyboard of a laptop to write the code, then you may have felt the need of pressing the Fn key for pressing the Function keys, like F11. Note that there are multiple uses of a function key on your laptop, for which the Fn key needs to be pressed in combination with the keys from F1 – F12. Several laptops come with a feature where the Fn can be locked. This causes the Function keys to act as the primary keys, so they do not need to be pressed with the Fn key to activate.

4. **Worksheet Intellisense Menu:** The Intellisense menu is a drop down menu comprising of words that are predefined for your help. Upon typing the period symbol (.), you can see this menu activating in the editor of Visual Basic. However, it does not always work. A case where it does not work is while working with property of worksheets. If you press Worksheets("Sheet1"), it will not show up the Intellisense menu. This can frustrate some users, as they may think that it is some kind of a glitch.

However, this happens because the worksheets property consists of various references to multiple sheets. Based on the references, methods and properties varying for each of the cases. Note that the Intellisense is not so intelligent that it can identify the period symbol there. This frustration has to be coped with until some update comes in the application to deal with it. Nevertheless, you can use the following two ways to avoid this issue and find the Intellisense dropdown menu for worksheets as well.

- You can use the worksheets codename that you are referencing. This technique is quite easy as it can help in bringing the menu out. This works because the code does not break if the user wishes to change the name of the sheet.

- The second way is by first setting the worksheet you want to work on as a variable in the Worksheets object. After that, whenever you will type the name of the variable assigned to your worksheet, with a period after that, it will show up the Intellisense menu.

5. **Free Use of Comments:** As explained earlier, comments can be helpful in understanding the created or modified codes in a macro. It also helps in understanding the purpose of a code in the macro. It was explained earlier that a comment can be started with the apostrophe mark ('). As soon as you move the cursor away from the comment line, the text in the line will change to green color. That way, you will know that it is a comment and it will be easier for you to differentiate it with the rest of the code. Note that VBA will avoid reading all comments that are starting with the apostrophe mark. There is no limit to the usage of comments in the editor window.

   But, note that comments are still not that widely used by expert VBA developers. They believe that the code itself is able to give full explanation of what the code is doing. So, they believe that adding a comment is useless. However, this may not be applicable to all types of users. Beginners can get help with visible comments to understand the code. Some other reasons for the significance of comments are:

   - Upon arriving back to an existing piece of macro code later, it is possible that you may not remember the purpose of a created macro. With comments, you can at least provide various sections of the code with headings that will define their purpose. It makes it quite easy, at least for cases where the macro code is lengthy. In addition, it will help in utilizing the complete code at any time at a much faster rate.

- Sometimes, users or developers share their VB project codes with other developers or users for various objectives. For the person who has not written the code, it can be a great advantage to understand what the code is doing with the help of mentioned comments.

6. **Using F8 For Stepping Via Each Code Line:** For stepping through every code line, we use the keyboard key F8. This shortcut key is applicable in Mac computers with the combination: Cmd + Shift + I. With this shortcut key, you can debug and test each code line in your created macros. Additionally, you can access Excel along with the editor screen to check the performance of each line executing on the screen. This is more feasible when you use a dual-monitor system.

   This can be of great advantage in situations where you want to keep testing each line for errors side by side. For using the Through or Step Into shortcut, you can follow the below steps:

   - Click within the macro you want to execute. You can click on the code line that you want to step into. The line will start at the top.

   - Press the F8 key.

   - It will highlight the macro name in yellow color.

   - Press F8 again after it to compile the code line. This will then highlight the line after it.

   - Keep pressing the F8 key to compile each line.

   Note that the lines that are highlighted on every step are not executed until the F8 key is pressed again.

7. **Assigning Macros To Various Shapes:** It may seem an outdated layout for using sheet controls for various buttons that run macros. Fortunately, the use of shapes is also applicable in Excel to execute macros. You can format or color these shapes to make them look like buttons in your sheet. Here is the method to assign various shapes to your macros:

    - Add a shape on your sheet. Format it the way you prefer it. You can change the shape to circular or rectangular as per your preference.
    - After that, press right click on the shape you selected and click on the "Assign Macro" option.
    - Select the relevant macro that you want from the list provided and press OK. Normally, this macro is the same one that is stored with the same shape as you have decided for yours to be.
    - Click the shape by selecting a cell from your worksheet.
    - When you move your mouse cursor over the shape, you will see that your mouse cursor changes to a hand. This indicates that you can perform an action with the shape. In this case it will execute the macro assigned to it.

    Note that it is prudent that you have a message box option present there with a Yes or No button to ask you if you want to run the macro. This is helpful in preventing the execution of an unnecessary macro.

8. **Utilize the For Next Loop For Running Repetitive Tasks Automatically:** Excel macros have been designed for a significant purpose, which is to perform tasks that need to be repeated again and again. Such tasks include copying workbook data from one to multiple workbooks, setting up filters for every pivot table,

developing lists in sheets, formatting several sheets, etc. Note that loops are of high significance in VB applications. Their purpose is to automatically run certain tasks assigned to them. It helps in looping a certain set of instruction until the tasks fulfills the purpose completely.

As mentioned earlier, several types of loops exist that have been used in various programming languages. The For Next loop is the most common of them all. You can learn about loops in detail from various online sources.

9. **Utilizing Option Explicit:** Many developers avoid using it, but it is still a recommended tip that you can use for its advantages. You can use Option Explicit for declaring variables. It is a way of preventing typos for various variable names in the VBE. Declaring variables and avoiding unnecessary tokenizing has already been discussed in previous chapters.

   With Option Explicit, you are instructing VBA to develop a variable and save it within the memory to make it accessible at later stages while running a code. As variables are saved beforehand, you can use the variable without making any typos and save some time while writing the code and repeating the variable name. Any undeclared variable will be prompted by the VBE with a compiler error that says "Variable Not Defined." It will also show the undeclared variable so that you can fix the typo without the need of searching for it. If your Option Explicit function is turned off, you may still end up with errors upon typing a misspelled variable. But, it can be difficult to locate the error in a lengthy macro without Option Explicit function turned on. So, try using it while you write your code. To turn it on, just type "Option Explicit" on the top of the module. VBE may automate it for you if you go to Tools -> Options -> and ticking the "Require Variable Declaration" box. You can see the words Option Explicit written on top of your module for writing the code to know that it is turned on.

10. **Utilizing the Excel Tables or ListObjects:** Several advantages exist that support the effective role of Excel Tables in workbooks. You can reduce the amount of time spent with these by automatically filling columns, sourcing data for pivot tables, and formatting them. With Excel tables, the VBA code is much easier to write specifically for dynamic data. We refer to it as dynamic, as it keeps updating itself depending upon the addition of new data set or list in the row or columns of the worksheets. You can have plenty of instances where the use of Excel tables is needed. For that ListObjects is used in the code to create the necessary operation for modifying the table as you progress with the data input. Note that Excel tables let you update the list even when a data is removed from the list in the table.

11. **Using Macro Recorder:** This feature is unique to Excel and VBA applications. Upon running it, it will start creating VBA code in MS Excel. For instance, upon turning it on, you can perform your usual tasks in Excel, like writing formulae or copy/pasting text. Meanwhile, Macro recorder will start creating the relevant code for your actions and save it to the module for code in the project window.

    This outstanding tool is great for beginners as it helps in understanding how the code is being created for your macro actions. It gives you snippets of the code and understanding from time to time. Note that the object model of Excel is so vast that it is almost impossible to learn all the methods, object references, and properties present in it. Thus, using a Macro recorder can help in accessing some of the code for your objects, shapes, lists, slicers, pivot tables, etc., that you frequently use in your workbooks.

However, there are some restrictions with Macro recorders. It will not add any code snippets for message boxes, If commands, errors/typos, loops, etc. For those, the user will have to create the code on his or her own by learning these advanced methods. These methods will enable you to understand the complete VB coding language for creating macros efficiently.

12. **Immediate Window:** This window lets Visual Basic editor to execute each code line separately. You have the ability to execute a technique related to an object or return the code output on the Immediate Window. For instance, you have a task to locate the number of worksheets in a particular workbook. For that, you can ask the window a question in VBA code, like:

    ?Worksheets.Count

    Upon pressing enter, your query gets addressed with its answer in the following line. You can also use Immediate Window for debugging code lines with the help of Debug.Print technique. Furthermore, you can access this window with the shortcut key: Ctrl + G.

13. **Macros Keyboard Shortcuts Assignment:** You are already familiar with this technique, as it had been discussed in one of the previous chapters. Nevertheless, it does not hurt to revisit it once again as it is an important function to help you assign shortcuts for your created macros. You can use the Macro Options window to access the area for assigning the key for it.

    - Press the button for Macros located in the Developer option or you can also access it from the View option present in the ribbon.

    - Select the file that consists of the macro from the dropdown menu present in the Macros Options box.

- Select the macros from the list and press the button saying “Options.”
- Type the letter for which you want to assign your developed macros. As mentioned earlier, you can create a complex combination to avoid any overriding of the shortcut keys for some other operation. It is always advisable to select a key with the Shift key to make it a unique combination.
- Press the OK button once you have assigned the keys.
- After that, you can access your macros by pressing the shortcut key linked to it and use it.

14. **Checking Whether A Selected Range Is Present Or Not:** Several times, you may face a situation where a range of cells have to be identified whether they are selected or not. This is needed to be done prior to running a macro. In some situations, they may have a shape, like a slicer, a chart, etc., selected for them, then it can cause an error in the macro code.

    For example, a code is there to delete rows that are blank in a chosen range of cells. For running a macro normally, you will have to first choose a range for the code to work. The following code will help in verifying whether the range is chosen or not:

    ‘For checking if a range is chosen

    If TypeName(Selection) <> “Range” Then MsgBox “Please choose a range beforehand.”, vbOKOnly, “Select Range”

    Exit Sub

    End If

In this code, a name of the object or data type will be returned by the function TypeName for the provided objects or variables. In the above case, it will check for the Selection and return the object types selected there. If a range is not selected, then the If statement will serve its purpose. Usually, this code needs to be added above the macro. If there is no range selected, then a pop-up box appears on the screen that will suggest the user to first select a range. As usual, the Exit Sub statement will end the macro.

15. **Ctrl + Y (Deletes a Code Line):** This useful tool in VBE is there to remove any lines that your editor cursor is actively highlighting. This can be a little confusing for some, as Ctrl + Y is a shortcut key that has been universally used for redoing an operation in an application, even in Excel. If you check the menu for Edit in your Excel, you will see that the Redo command does not have any shortcut key assigned to it. Alternatively, for Redo, you can use Alt + R or Alt + E for redoing. However, in the VBE editor, you can use Ctrl + Y to delete a line.

16. **Using Ctrl + i To Access Quick Info:** This significant keyboard shortcut is there to help with various tips and short notes on what the various methods, functions, and properties are used for. To use it, you can press the Ctrl + i buttons, which you can do like this:

    - Highlight the cursor on the relevant text or word that you want to look information for.
    - After that, press the Ctrl + i keys.
    - You will then see a screen next to the text.
    - You can press the Esc button to close the window or you can simply move your cursor from that text.

If there is a variable chosen within the code line that you wish to see information for (specifically for its parameters, instead of the variable's value or the type of data it has), then you can press the key combination Ctrl + Shift + i to look at the information for the parameter.

17. **Ctrl + j For Using Intellisense dropdown menu:** Intellisense menu was discussed previously so you know what it is used for. You can use it for displaying methods, objects, properties, etc. after you type the period symbol (.). However, sometimes you want to revisit a particular line to view the Intellisense menu for that particular object. For that you can press the Ctrl + J keys to view the menu. Alternatively, you can simply type that line again to reopen the Intellisense menu for that particular line.

    Furthermore, you can press the combination keys Ctrl + J to choose the various variables from the dropdown list. Sometimes, a user may select a wrong variable, for which he or she needs to alter the name. Pressing the Ctrl + J keys will offer a list of variable names for that when the cursor is highlighted over that particular mistyped variable. In addition, prefixing a variable name will close the other variable from the list.

18. **Worksheet Functions:** Several functions in the worksheet can also be utilized in your workbook in Excel. You can use these functions in various formulae in Excel, like min, max, countif, vlookup, match, etc. For this, you need to type WorksheetFunction., in the editor for macro, and you can then view all the functions that are provided to you in Visual Basic applications.

    You can think of worksheet functions as a live example that shows how the efficiency of Excel combines with the usability of VBA code. Note that upon using it, you will be provided with the list of arguments, but not their names. So, you will have to type the formula for it in Excel to determine the type of argument, unless you have already memorized them.

While it may vary from user to user, yet Match is the most prominently used function of worksheet in VBA. It can be used for finding a value and returning a column or row number that this matched value indicates. For some, it can be an easier alternative to Range.Find technique.

Understanding Absolute and Relative Macro Recording

Now that you have attuned yourself to the basics of Macros and got a little glimpse of Macro recording, it is now time to delve a little deeper. We are now going to understand how you can begin recording macros.

Before you get started, let us understand an essential point: Excel provides you with two modes for the purpose of recording. These two modes are absolute reference and relative reference.

Let us try to find out how we can work these two modes.

Mode One: Recording with Absolute References

By default, you will be using absolute reference when you start working with recording macros. When we use the term 'absolute reference', then we are using it in the context of cell references that are discovered in formulas. What this means is that when a cell reference in a particular formula has an absolute reference, then it does not modify itself automatically when you paste the cell into a new area of the Excel sheet.

Perhaps the best way to understand this is by actually putting the entire concept into practice. So let us get right to it.

Let us first create a chart in excel.

	A	B	C	D	E	F	G	H
1		**Region**	**Target**	**Branch**				
2		USA	New York	01234				
3		USA	New York	12341				
4		USA	New York	23544				
5		USA	New York	73568				
6		Asia	Shanghai	94678				
7		Asia	Shanghai	25208				
8		Asia	Shanghai	24621				
9								

Now let us get down to recording the macro.

1. The first thing that you should make sure is that you have the A1 cell selected.

2. Head over to the Developer tab and then select Record Macro.

3. You will now be prompted to give a name for the macro. For the purpose of this example, we are going to go right ahead and name the macro as "AddTotal". Not very imaginative, but if you like, we could also go with "TotalRecall". It's your choice.

4. Next, select This Workbook for the location of the save.

5. Then click on OK to begin recording. From this point onwards, Excel is going to record everything you do. So let us get started on the below steps.

6. Select cell A9 and enter 'Total' into the field.

7. Once you have entered Total into A9, select the cell D9 and then type this formula: =COUNTA(D2:D8). This gives you a total of the branch numbers in the box that you have selected (which would be D9). The reason why we use COUNTA is because the branch numbers are actually stored as text.

8. Now head back to the Developer tab and select the Stop Recording option to stop the recording process.

Now the final sheet should look something like the below:

	A	B	C	D	E	F	G	H
1		**Region**	**Target**	**Branch**				
2		USA	New York	01234				
3		USA	New York	12341				
4		USA	New York	23544				
5		USA	New York	73568				
6		Asia	Shanghai	94678				

7		Asia	Shanghai	25208				
8		Asia	Shanghai	24621				
9	Total			7				

Now here is where the incredible happens. If you would like to view your macro, then all you have to do is delete the total row (which would be Row 9). Then you simply have to follow the below steps:

1. Go to the Developer tab and then select Macros
2. You should now look for the "AddTotal" macro (or the "TotalRecall" macro, depending on how you named it).
3. When you find it, click on the run button.

If everything goes well with Excel, you should now be able to see your actions played back. You will notice that your table will now have a total.

Now let us expand the above example and add another table right next to it.

	A	B	C	D	E	F	G	H
1		**Region**	**Target**	**Branch**		**Region**	**Target**	**Branch**
2		USA	New York	01234		Europe	Amsterdam	63845
3		USA	New York	12341		Europe	Amsterdam	71134
4		USA	New York	23544		Europe	Amsterdam	05730

5		USA	New York	73568		Europe	Amsterdam	48593
6		Asia	Shanghai	94678		Russia	Moscow	16344
7		Asia	Shanghai	25208		Russia	Moscow	64364
8		Asia	Shanghai	24621		Russia	Moscow	55435
9	Total			7				

You have two tables.

At this point, now matter what you do or how hard you try, you cannot make the macro function properly for the second table.

If you are wondering why, then this is the reason: you recorded it as an absolute macro.

Confused? Don't be.

Let us look at what this means by examining the code of the macro that we just created.

To do that, we now head back over to the Developer tab and then we select Macros. A dialog box will now open that shows all the macros that you have created. At this point, you should have just one macro and that would be the "AddTotal" or "TotalRecall" macro.

Go right ahead and select the macro that oy have created. Click on the Edit button. A new window will open up. This is your Visual Basic Editor window.

You might see a code that looks something like this.

Sub AddTotal()

Range("A9").Select

ActiveCell.FormulaR1C1 = "Total"

Range("D9").Select

ActiveCell.FormulaR1C1 = "=COUNTA(R[-7]C:R[-1]C)"

End Sub

Look closely at lines two and four of the code. What do you notice? Rather, what columns have you mentioned in the code? It shows A and D right?

When you gave Excel the command to simply choose the range of cells ending at A9 and D9, that is exactly what Excel did. When you select A9, then you get A9 and no other cell. Which is why it is difficult to simply replicate the result on another cell. It simply cannot happen.

Now what happens if we try to record the macro by using the relative reference option? Let us find out.

Mode Two: Recording with Relative References

When you use the option of Relative References, then Excel basically understands it as relative to the active cell you are working on.

This is why, you need to be more careful with your cell choice, both when you are recording the relative reference and when you are done recording to run the macro.

The first thing we are going to do is set up the table. Ideally, we are going to use the same table we used for the Absolute Reference example.

If you have not already, then here is the table for your use.

	A	B	C	D	E	F	G	H
1		**Region**	**Target**	**Branch**		**Region**	**Target**	**Branch**
2		USA	New York	01234		Europe	Amsterdam	63845
3		USA	New York	12341		Europe	Amsterdam	71134
4		USA	New York	23544		Europe	Amsterdam	05730
5		USA	New York	73568		Europe	Amsterdam	48593
6		Asia	Shanghai	94678		Russia	Moscow	16344
7		Asia	Shanghai	25208		Russia	Moscow	64364
8		Asia	Shanghai	24621		Russia	Moscow	55435
9								

Once the table has been set up, follow the below steps to work on it.

1. Head over toe the Developer tab and then select the Use Relative References option.

2. Before you begin the recording, make sure that you have selected the A1 cell.

3. Back to the Developer tab. Choose the Record Macro option.

4. Now we have to name to the macro. For the purpose of this example, we can use the name "AddRelative". However, you can use a name that you would like.

5. Next, you have to select This Workbook option as the save location.

6. Once you have done so, click on OK to begin your location.

7. Just like with the example with Absolute Reference, select the cell A9 and type in Total.

8. Now we are going to go to cell D9 and type in the following command: =COUNTA(D2:D8)

9. Head over to the Developer tab and then select the Stop Recording option. This will end the recording of Absolute Reference mode.

Once you have completed the recording, we are going to examine the code and find out just what happened.

To do that, we once again head back to the Developer tab and then select Macros. You will notice a list of macros here. If you have been following the tutorial strictly, then you should be able to notice two different macros. One should be for the Absolute Reference macro while the other should be for the Relative Reference. You should select the macro for the Relative Reference (which is named "AddRelative" in this case).

Click the Edit button to see a block of code that should look like this.

```
Sub AddRelative()

ActiveCell.Offset(9, 0).Range("A1").Select

ActiveCell.FormulaR1C1 = "Total"

ActiveCell.Offset(0, 3).Range("A1").Select

ActiveCell.FormulaR1C1 = "=COUNTA(R[-7]C:R[-1]C)"

End Sub
```

When you look the code, the changes will be rather obvious. At this point, you cannot see a specific cell being mentioned in the code at all.

Rather, if you look at line 2, then you will notice that the code features a unique property that appears in the form of an OFFSET command. When Excel reads this command, it basically does not fix on a particular cell.

What does OFFSET command actually mean and what does it tell Excel to do for you?

Offset is basically the property of Excel to shift to a specific number of cells from the starting cell, either in a vertical position (along columns) or in a horizontal position (along rows). This means that the command tells Excel to move a particular number of spots.

Let us look at the example above and use the explanation to find out what is happening.

In the code for Relative Reference, Excel is move 9 cells in the row. It will move 0 columns sideways. Basically, Excel is going to remain in the A1 column and move downwards.

Time to see the macro being played.

In order to do this, we are going to follow similar steps as the ones followed for Absolute Reference.

1. Click on cell A1
2. Go to the Developer tab and then select Macros.
3. You should now look for the "AddRelative" macro or whatever name you have given to the Relative Reference macro.
4. Click Run
5. Now, go over to cell F1

6. We are going to repeat the steps above so go the Developer Tab and select Macros
7. Select the "AddRelative" macro or the name that you have given to this macro.
8. Click on the Run button

You will notice that the macro not only runs on the first table, but also the second table created in the Excel sheet. This is because, unlike Absolute Reference, you are not entering a command that specifies a particular cell number. This means that the macro does not attach itself to certain cells. You are only telling the macro to work in relation to the cells that it has and the command it has been given.

Think of the above concept this way. You have given a map to a person. You have told the person to head straight and then take a left using a certain streets and those streets only. That is Absolute Reference.

You are now telling the person to head straight and then take a left, but you are giving the person general directions without forcing him or her to follow a particular street. That is Relative Reference.

The one thing that you have to make sure is that when you are working with Relative Reference, you have to select the right cell before you run the program.

Additionally, you have to ensure that the section of data that you want to focus on has the same number of rows and columns as the original section.

In the above example, columns A to D were the original sections. They had eight rows of data (one row for titles and the remaining seven rows for data). The next sections that we had focused on were columns E to H, which also had the same number of rows.

This is how macro recording works with both Absolute Reference and Rclative Reference.

Here are a few points to remember when working with Excel macros.

1. Starting with Excel 2007, you now have the option to save worksheets that contains macros with a new file name. When you are using Excel 2010 for example, then you typically save the file using the .xlsx extension. When you save the file in that extension, you cannot save the macros as well. What happens to the macros? Excel removes all macros from the sheet if the sheet is saved using .xlsx extension. Which is why, you are now giving an option to save the sheet as an Excel Macro-Enabled Workbook. When you do this, the sheet gets a different extension, the .xlsm extension. The main reason for doing this is so that .xlsx does not contain any coding and hence is safe to open. However, a .xlsm file may contain coding that could harm your computer. The distinction in file extensions are made so that you can decide if you trust the source of the document to open it.

2. Another feature that you might notice with Excel 2010 (and future versions) is the upgrade in the Office security. One of the components of the Office security is the concept of trusted documents. What this means is that you are confident about the document to run macros in it. When you open a sheet that contains macros in it, then you might notice a message that pops up within a ribbon on top of the sheet that says that macros has been disabled. The way to enable the macros is by pressing the Enable button. Once you do that, the sheet remembers the action and the next time you open the sheet, you won't have to click on the Enable button again. Essentially, what you have done is give the command to the sheet that you trust the content and the macros within it. When

you are working with clients or with your colleagues, then this feature becomes important for two reasons:

a. You get to decide if you trust the source of the content.

b. You only have to Enable the macros once. This means that all the people working on the sheet are not annoyed by the constant message that the macros are disabled that pops up each time the sheet is open.

3. Sometimes, when you create macros, then you might want to have an easy way to run them. Fortunately, Excel has a solution for that. What you can do is assign a macro button to help you create a user interface called form controls to work with your macros. Sounds convenient? Then let us look at how you can activate this button. There are numerous types of form controls. You can choose to use buttons (which are commonly used as the controls) or you can choose to add scrollbars. Let us go back to the example we had used before and try to add a button to the macro. Here is how it is done:

    a. Head over to the Developer tab and then choose the Insert button.

    b. In the drop-down list that appears, click on the button Form Control option.

    c. Click on the location where you would like to place the button. When you place the button control into your sheet, a special box called the Assign Macros dialog box appears on the sheet. You can then assign a macro to that button.

    d. At this point, we have two macros – "AddTotal" and "AddRelative" – in the list of macros. Choose any one of them and assign them.

    e. You are now ready to use the buttons!

CHAPTER 12

Executing A Macro Upon Modification Of Some Cells In Excel

You already know that by now that MS Excel can be used for developing macros, which are only accessible when a value is entered in a particular cell of a worksheet or sheet, which is open at that moment. Be aware that calling macros for no reason will only slow the speed of your sheet and lower its performance.

In several instances, the macro executes only when there is an entered value in the sheet cells. You need to make sure whether the ActiveCell is such an element. For that, you will need to use the Intersect method on the cell range and the ActiveCell for verification of the currently active cell as being part of the specified range. If the ActiveCell is present within the range, and has the key cells present in it, then the macro will be called. For this, the VB macro will be created in the following way:

1. First, you will right click in the Project window on the tab for Sheet1, and after that click on the ViewCode option. Upon doing so, you will see the Module sheet open behind the tab for Sheet1.

2. You will then have to type the following code in the VBE.

Private Sub Worksheet_Change(ByVal Target As Range)

Dim KeyCells As Range

'KeyCells is the variable that consists of cells, which will send a notification upon altering a value in them.

Set KeyCells Range("A1:C10")

*If Not Application.Intersect(KeyCells, Range(Target.Address))_*

Is Nothing Then

'This displays a message upon changing one of the specific cells.

MsgBox "Cell" & Target.Adress & "has been altered."

End If

End Sub

3. After that, you have to click on the option saying close and return to MS Excel that you can find in the File tab menu.

Handling and Trapping Macro Errors

You will need to add the program lines in all the macros for processing and intercepting any error when they occur in the code. You can frequently witness errors occurring in the macro when it is executing. This can be due to several reasons, like typos in the code and execution of a macro in scenarios that it was not programmed to run in the first place.

If you add an error trapping function to your macro, you will know the output due to an error. You will have the power to regulate the error occurring in the code. Thus, you have the authority to take the necessary steps to handle it without being confused about what could be wrong with your code.

If you fail to include an error handling function in your code, then it could lead to an irrelevant behavior by your Excel. The worst that can happen due to this mess is that the other users may not be able to see the latest changes in your worksheets. Plus, Excel might also freeze in such a case and there can be loss of data due to it. Plus, all these issues can even occur at once, leading to a more cumbersome situation.

Note that you want other users to not leave their own reaction to various error messages that may occur in your work. For instance,

A Run-time error '513' may return that can cause an error message saying:

"Application-defined or object-defined error"

Thus, you are going to need the help of error handling functions to execute the necessary steps beforehand, and without any other user's involvement.

Basic Error Handling Function

You can find several ways to add a code for error handling actions in your macro. You can study the following code, which is one such example.

Sub MacroName()

On Error GoTo errHandler

Macro code

ProcDone:

```
Exit Sub

errHandler:

MsgBox Err.Number & ":" & Err.Description

Resume procDone

End Sub
```

With the on Error line of code present in the above VBA program, you are turning on the error trapping function. This code will offer a tracking system for all the errors that may occur in a macro. The error will be returned in the VBA object known as Err. If an error occurs in the code, the statement: "On Error Goto errHandler," Excel will instruct the macro to stop running the operation. It will then move to the errHandler statement from where it will continue with the necessary operations.

With the MSGBox statement, a message will be displayed on the screen that provides with information related to the error occurred. Err.Number is the identification number provided for the particular error object, which is taken from the library for VBA errors. Furthermore, the Err.Description statement decribes the error. With procDone, the macro will continue running the statement label procDone.

Refined Codes For Error Handling

Let's make an assumption that you have added the code for error handling in your macro discussed in the previous section. Upon evaluating the macro, an error takes place. So, you get a message displayed that lets you known the nature and number of the occurred error. You will have to carry a revision with the error handler in response to the particular error faced. In the example provided, the error that occurs is 1234.

```
Sub MacroName()


On Error Goto errHandler

Macro code

procDone:

Exit Sub

errHandler:

Select Case Err.Number

Case 1234

Error handling code for error 1234

Case Else

'Every error outstanding

MsgBox Err.Number & ":" & Err.Description

End Select

Resume procDone

End Sub
```

Upon testing the macro to check for other errors that may be possible in the code, you may want to extend the functionality of the Select case command along with other suitable cases for this code. The following code will offer you a refined messages for your macro:

```
Sub MacroName()

On Error Goto errHandler

Dim msg$, title$, icon&

Macro code

procDone:

Exit Sub

errHandler:

icon& = vbOKOnly +vbCritical

Select Case Err.Number

Case 53

title$ = “File Missing”

msg$ = “Macro unable to find the necessary file.”

msg$ = msg$  vbNewline & vbNewLine

msg$ = msg$ & “Please inform this to the developer.”

Case Else

Title$ = “Error not anticipated”

msg$ = Err.Number  “:” & Err.Description

msg$ = msg$ & vbNewline  vbNewLine

msg$ = msg$ & “Please note down this message”
```

```
End Select

MsgBox Err.Number & ":" & Err.Description

Resume procDone

End Sub
```

Macro Debugging

The Debug Button and the Error Message Notification

While you are executing a macro, you will occasionally run into an error message that says: "Run-time Error," followed by an error message. You can find three types of buttons available on the box for the error message. These are: Debug, Help, and End.

You can stop the macro when facing error with the End button present on the error box. If you want to access more information about the error, then you can press the Help button. Pressing the Help button will take you to a MS site that has a list of possible reasons behind the error that has occurred. You will also have the relevant solutions for each of the errors specified there. For solving the issue, you can choose the Debug button, which then takes you to the Visual basic editor.

Conclusion

People have a misconception about macros; they think that to get started, you might need the knowledge of advanced coding. Here is the reality; while coding is an integral part of macros, it does not mean that you will be spending endless hours trying to go through the basics of coding and then trying to master its complex forms.

One of the things that makes macros convenient to work with is the fact that you – like anybody else – can pick up the fundamentals and then get started on it.

But apart from the above advice, let me share a few tips that you might find useful while you are working on Excel macros.

1. My recommendation would be to always begin from the home position. This makes it easier to you to plot your data and create macros for them. It help you create additional tables as compared to the first one or in relation to it. In order to start from the home position, all you have to do is hit CTRL + Home.

2. If you would like to navigate, make sure you are using the directional keys. Once you start begin working on macros, you are going to have a lot of data to look through. Scrolling would mean that you are going to skip data that you require. Your navigation should be fixed to Up, Down, Left, Right, and the End keys.

3. This is an important tip and it is one even professionals with years of experience tend to commit. Create small macros that cater to specific function. Let us understand this tip with the help of an example. If you would like to sort through the data, then create a macro for it. If you then decide to take information from the data, then create a separate macro for it. Do not combine all your macros for two vital reasons:

    a. If you combine various tasks into one macro, then your macro ends up running slower. The more you add into a macro, the slower it runs. Initially, this might not be a problem but when you begin to add more formations and complex information, then you are really going to feel the slow pace of the process.

    b. Secondly, we are all capable of making mistakes. This means that often, a macro might end up having an error and won't run properly. In such situations, you should be able to figure out which task of a macro is causing the problem and fix it. The task of identifying a problem becomes difficult if you group different tasks into one macro. You might end up looking through each and every line of code to find out where the problem lies. If you have a small macro, this might not be a problem. But if you end up having many lines of code, then you are going to spend a lot of time trying to find out the problem.

4. When you have fixed information or fixed data, make sure you enter it in advance before you start working on variable data. Let us assume that you have a column called "City". You are working on only one city, which is "New York". In that case, make sure you fill up the column with New York before beginning on any macro. That way, you save the precious time

filling up each and every cell with the same entry and second, you won't have to run macro each time you create the same entry. Macros are effective when they are used for complex tasks and working with different sets of data. It becomes pointless when you are merely using it for the same data repeatedly.

5. Take advantage of keyboard shortcuts. It might be a little cumbersome working with the shortcuts when you start, but once you get the hang of it, you won't have any problems with the shortcuts at all. For example, if you would like to highlight a specific column, then all you have to do is hold down the END key, and the hit SHIFT + DOWN key. The entire column will be highlighted for you without changing anything within the macro.

6. Remember that if you do not enter the keystrokes as recommended by Excel, then your macro is bound to fail. This is why, you have to make sure that you get your keystrokes right. Take the time to learn some of the shortcuts and key combinations before working on your macro.

7. If you would like to know the shortcuts to the menus, then all you have to do is hit the ALT key while inside the sheet. This will display the menu shortcuts. Once you have made note of the shortcuts, hit the ALT key again and then the shortcut highlights will disappear.

8. If you would like to separate names within a sheet from one column into two, then there is an easy way to go about it. The first thing you have to do is CTRL + HOME and then press CTRL + A. Once that is done, head over to Data and the select Text to Columns. In the first dialog box that appears, click on the Delimited and then click on Next. In the next window that opens up, you have to choose the character that delimits your

text. We know that the common character between the first and last name is Space. So check on the option that says Space and then click Next. Finally, in the last box, choose the option Text and hit Finish. Once you perform the above actions, your names will be split into two columns.

With that, I hope you are ready to begin your macros journey. Enjoy the process and hope macros brings a world of convenience to your Excel workings.

References

Add your personal Excel Macros to the ribbon. (2019). Retrieved from https://www.get-digital-help.com/2013/12/03/add-your-personal-excel-macros-to-the-ribbon/

Chandran, M. (2019). How to run macro based on cell value in Excel?. Retrieved from https://www.extendoffice.com/documents/excel/4420-excel-run-macro-based-on-cell-value.html

Create a button for a macro - HowTo-Outlook. (2019). Retrieved from https://www.howto-outlook.com/howto/macrobutton.htm

How to Build a Custom Excel Toolbar of VBA Macros. (2019). Retrieved from https://www.makeuseof.com/tag/custom-excel-toolbar-vba-macros/

How to Call or Run a Another Macro From a Macro - Excel Campus. (2019). Retrieved from https://www.excelcampus.com/library/vba-call-statement-run-macro-from-macro/

How to Optimize VBA Performance. (2019). Retrieved from https://www.spreadsheet1.com/how-to-optimize-vba-performance.html

Optimize Slow VBA Code. Speed Up Efficient VBA Code/Macros. (2019). Retrieved from https://www.ozgrid.com/VBA/SpeedingUpVBACode.htm

Shepherd, R. (2004). Excel VBA macro programming. New York: McGraw-Hill/Osborne.

Troy, A., & Gonzalez, J. (2006). Office VBA macros you can use today. Uniontown: Holy Macro! Books.

Walkenbach ... (2013). Excel 2003 Power Programming with VBA. Hoboken: Wiley.

Walkenbach, J. (2004). Excel VBA Programming For Dummies. John Wiley & Sons.

Made in the USA
Columbia, SC
11 November 2020